Just a *Little* Bit More *Faith*

Just a *Little* Bit More *Faith*

How to Walk and not Faint

ANGELA COLBERT

Library of Congress Control Number: 2024903365

ISBN: 979-8-89228-130-0   (Paperback)
ISBN: 979-8-89228-131-7   (Hardcover)
ISBN: 979-8-89228-132-4   (eBook)

Printed in the United States of America

CONTENTS

Introduction vii

Chapter 1   Faith in Purpose...1
Chapter 2   The Pruning..7
Chapter 3   Faith Walk..26
Chapter 4   Faith in the New Age...................................35
Chapter 5   What Do We Know about Faith?...................46
Chapter 6   Faith and the Concerns of Life...................56
Chapter 7   Our Faith and God's Faithfulness 69
Chapter 8   How to Increase Your Faith 79

Conclusion..89
Resources 91

INTRODUCTION

My self-actualization journey took me more than six years to complete. This was a personal journey that was filled with torment. By the time I found out that it was God, I had gone through countless days and nights of no sleep, no food, and no understanding. I had to come to the realization that time was winding down, and God wanted me to completely give myself to him.

You see, I had known God from an early age, but I also knew the world. I believe that the moment Satan found out about my relationship with God, I became a target. I am not blaming Satan for my mistakes. I take complete responsibility for them all, but he was there in the midst smiling and speculating.

I took away someone's livelihood. I took it away by an act of omission. I never told them what had taken place. I hoped and prayed that everything would turn out okay—a fantasy. Not that praying isn't good, but in this situation, I should have told her the reality of the situation. I mixed all this with drugs, alcohol, and fear. The fear came from not knowing how to say what I had to say. This made me want to shrink into more and more abuse whenever I thought about it.

To me, it seemed as if God said, "Don't come to me now wanting me to make a miracle from your mess. You know exactly what you should have done." I might add that the person I let this happen to didn't exactly accept it.

My torment was so bad that I lost an enormous amount of weight and self-respect. Right now, I'll just tell you that my journey to relieve myself of this torment took me to places I never would have dreamed I would even imagine going.

When you go through hell, you might be willing to try just about anything. It seemed as if my prayers were not being answered, so I searched the Internet and listened to countless gurus on several subjects.

I turned to New Age beliefs and learned a great deal. I learned that no matter what goes on in my life, God will be there trying to guide me back into the fold. As deep as I got into New Age philosophies, the more I began to hear God's voice. I heard it in other people, I heard it in secular music, I heard it while watching movies, and then I heard it in my dreams. I also heard Him say that New Age was not the way. He is the only way, and there is no substitute. Faith led me to the realization that everything in my life depends on the Lord and that I must depend on him. He knows what's best for us. When I was tired of running from his will, I had to say yes to it. He didn't take away the problem I feared most. He allowed it to happen, and he allowed the consequences to unfold. You might ask, why should I have faith then? He took away my drug and alcohol abuse and my self-degradation. He took away my doubts and showed me something much better; he showed me his love.

To do anything and get through it, I would simply have to have faith. Trouble will come, and sometimes, it will hang on for what may seem like forever. But with faith in God, all things are possible. That may seem like quite the cliché - but try it for yourself and let me know what you think.

Follow me as I take you through the faith journey.

Chapter 1

FAITH IN PURPOSE

The heart of man plans his way, the Lord establishes his steps.
Prov 16:9

Because God knows us by name, we can totally put our trust in him. We are not just numbers to him. He knows our most intimate thoughts, desires, and fears. He calls us friend. He is not the average friend either. The Bible says that there is no greater love than a friend who would lay down his life for another. Now, that is the kind of friend about whom he is talking. How do I know he means it? He sent his only begotten son to die for me and for you. At the same time the Bible says that we are adopted unto the Lord (Eph. 3:20).

Recently there have been scientific studies shown that God has even marked our DNA. Although I do not wholeheartedly subscribe to science as I will show in some parts of this book, I choose to believe that this is true. I choose to believe it because I know that he can do anything. For now, I will just say that God made sure that we would not get lost because he stamped our DNA.

I did say that I choose to believe the DNA findings were of God. I said this because Faith is a choice. It is a conscious choice that we all must make. We are not always going to have proof of everything right before our eyes but, what did Jesus say to Thomas? Jesus said to him, 'Have you believed since you have seen me? Blessed are those who have not seen and yet have believed." John 20:29.

I submit to you that everything in this life must take on a form of faith. We must believe that there will be air and that it will be breathable. We just trust in it even though we cannot see it. And then we look to find what is meaningful in this life. What do I do? Why am I here? I did not realize this but every few years people want to find out why they are here.

Several years ago, Rick Warren wrote The Purpose Driven Life. It was in 2002 to be exact. There was a cry from Christians again who wanted to know their purpose in life. The book told us that God had a plan or several plans for our lives when he created us. He suggests that the best way to find out our purpose or purposes is to seek the answer from the Creator. How many of us would want to go through life not fulfilling what God intended for us to do? Although God wants us to make the most of the gifts that he has instilled in each of us, we should try to find out what his plan for our lives is. How many of you know that this will take faith?

We must have faith that God will reveal his plans to us. We must have faith that it is God and not the enemy. In other words, we should have faith in the entire process. Knowing what God has in store for us makes things less complicated. If it is not a part of God's plan it can be canceled, it is as simple as that. Some people are all over the place, trying different things in life to create a self-reliant, successful life for themselves. For one thing, the term self-reliance should be deleted from all our vocabularies. God wants us to rely on him and not be self-reliant. I must admit that I have been in this struggle myself for several years. It wasn't until recently that I moved back home and found the Rick Warren book on the shelf. I remembered how the book sales were through the roof on it and how I had watched his interview with Oprah that I took it down and began to read it again.

Now I am looking at videos on different platforms and I am beginning to see this trend again with young people not knowing what their purpose is. Perhaps they were just born when the Purpose Driven Life was written. Who knows why they don't seek out this resource, but I am here to tell them right now that reading that book along with this one will help. Yes, these will help but I would be remiss if I didn't say that reading the Bible should be foremost in your lives.

First, we should begin to understand that God is in complete control of our lives. He controls the events of history. He is sovereign so there is no way that he is not aware. We make mistakes because we are human, but God does not. While he is moving in our lives, and we begin to have a stroke of fortune, this is God bringing us success. And yet when there is a stroke of misfortune, most of the time this is also God teaching us how to put our trust in him. We are not alone in this world. When the Bible says that God works together for the good of those who love him this is true. There is no such thing as luck.

The Bible says that God is a great rewarder for those who seek him. If he knocks and we open the door, he will come in and spend time with us. What will he show us that we may not have already known about ourselves? One thing that we were created for is to give God glory. We were also created to serve God. When we serve others, we serve God. "For I was hungry and you gave me food, I was thirsty and you gave me drink, I was a stranger and you welcomed me, I was naked and you clothed me, I was sick and you visited me, I was in prison, and you came to me.' Then the righteous will answer him, saying, 'Lord, when did we see you hungry and feed you, or thirsty and give you drink? And when did we see you a stranger and welcome you, or naked and clothe you? And when did we see you sick or in prison and visit you?' And the King will answer them, 'Truly, I say to you, as you did it to one of the least of these my brothers, you did it to me" (Matt 25:34-40).

I often find that when I am not doing something towards service that I become somewhat stagnated. Even if it is just something small, there should be something that we can do for others. You never know what will happen or who you will meet that God has placed there for such a time to impregnate your life with something maybe in the form of a career that you have been searching for.

This brings me to another point about our journeys. We can't be afraid when God gives us opportunities. Let me tell you a story. I was living in Seattle and traveling home to Louisiana one summer. I always knew I wanted to become a writer but, every time I wrote something I thought it wasn't good enough. This lasted several years. So, I asked God to help me. Give me a sign if this is what you want me to do. On one of the smaller flights into Louisiana, I happened to be sitting next a very nicely dressed woman. We exchanged pleasantries. She said that she was a writer and that she helps other writers. She hit her head on the overhead luggage compartment, and I helped her of course. You would think that this was my golden opportunity, right? I couldn't bring myself to ask if she would look at my work or that I wanted to become a writer myself. Fear had totally taken hold of me. I know it now as a ploy from Satan that has been working on me from birth. I felt like I let God down and myself. I have also learned not to worry too much about it because whatever God has for you will come to pass regardless of the letdowns. It can seemingly be over for you. You can be on skid row and if God said he wanted you to be an astronaut on that sealed scroll, that is the way it will be. You may not get there until you are sixty, but it will happen.

We were made for God's purpose. Yes, it is for his pleasure, but God is a good God. He created us and everything about him is good. He takes pleasure in our worship so much until he joins us in it. How wonderful is that?

Sure, I believe we can allow our journeys to be hindered. This is why we must allow the Lord to make a transformation in our lives. This is why we must draw close to him so that he will show us when the enemy has ulterior motives for things that happen. This time I stepped on my own feet through fear. It was another time in my life when I stepped on someone else's feet because of fear. It was my own fault, however. I allowed fear to cause me to make the wrong decisions. I must tell you that the war between good and evil is real and if God shows you any ounce of favor, Satan will find out. Satan can turn you into your own worst enemy. It is vital, especially now, that we cling to God and everything that is Holy so that he will direct our paths.

There is always much to do for others that will give God glory. We must be careful that we are not trying to use a tally when we do service for the Lord but, make sure that it is from a good place in our hearts. If we are not careful, we will end up doing things that we think will leave us with a big enough list entitled good things that will certainly speak for itself. Sorry, but we are saved by grace through faith and not our good works. Some people will say why do them then? Once you become transformed by the renewing of your mind you will want to with your whole heart and soul. You will want to please the Father. There were times when he was not pleased with us and wanted to destroy us. We want him to know that we are good and that we are worth his efforts.

When we decide to make God the center of our lives and to totally have faith in him, he will begin a good work in our lives. This good work will not only transform us, but it will show us what we should be doing for him and for ourselves. If we love God, we can be certain that He is working things out for our good (Rom 8:28)

The transformation will be cleansing so that we become Holy as he is. Nothing less than holy can enter heaven. You will notice during the transformation that you understand what you are reading in the Bible now. Yes, he will communicate differently, and I will tell you more about that later. God has made wonderful promises to us and if we keep his commandments, we will see them all while being shielded from corruption. What this means is that Satan will come but God will give us discernment and provide us with other weapons to use against the enemy.

For many things to take place God examines us and takes us through a journey that is sometimes not so pleasant. This journey, as I mentioned before, will be a transformation. When it is over, we shall come forth as pure gold (Job 23:10)

"For godly grief produces a repentance that leads to salvation without regret, whereas worldly grief produces death." 2 Cor 7:10.

Chapter 2

THE PRUNING

I am the true vine, and my Father is the vinedresser. Every branch in me that does not bear fruit he takes away, and every branch that does bear fruit he prunes, that it may bear more fruit. John 15:1–2

Brian arrived from work and noticed a wildly overgrown offshoot on his prized bougainvillea flowers that he had grown in his garden. The branch had been overgrown so much that it had started brushing aside the beauty of the flowers. As a person who cared for and loved the flowers, he thought the best thing he could do for them to blossom again was to hire a gardener to help chop them up, if not for anything else, at least for the inspiration and beauty the flowers added to his yard. Unfortunately, as the gardener started trimming the flowers, Brian became displeased; this was because the floor was littered with the branches and leaves from the flowers. He began to think that he had hired a terrible gardener.

He asked his wife, "Have you seen what the gardener is doing? He is trimming down everything. I don't think he knows his job." He became worried that the beauty he was trying to save was all gone. All the branches and flowers he cherished lay wilting on the ground.

Obviously, Brian never took any course in gardening because he knew little about how to tend and care for flowers. To his ignorant eyes, the gardener was a butcher who only destroyed his flowers;

but to the knowing eye, the gardener was a professional vinedresser. He did not know that a flower's life span increases with pruning.

When something unusual in life is discovered or after the blooming season, we welcome a moment to trim down all the unnecessary branches that may hinder our blossoming. This work is essentially the work of a gardener with gardening skills. To prune means to cut back or cut off parts for more profitable growth or to achieve a better shape. When this is done appropriately, we are encouraging healthy growth. Pruned plants will produce to their fullest potential. When pruning is neglected, we encourage overgrown and dead branches that hinder healthy growth. Although the plant may look bare when pruning is done, it is a means of preparing it for the best to come.

God is the master vinedresser, and this respect is what needs to be made known to the church in these last days. He wants believers to see and know him beyond a name they read in a book. He wants a personal experience that will produce conviction in the lives of individuals. That's why God began revealing this dimension to us so that we will come into alignment with his purpose and plans.

There were moments in the past when we only called on God for our needs, but this time, he is willing to reveal himself as a real God whom you can depend on and relate to more than someone close to you. That is why the Lord is doing the work of pruning us—so that we do not miss out on what he wants to do, even in this season.

But as it stands, it appears that men have built and are still building resistance and limiting the ever-available power of God. The vinedresser is willing to do his job, but the vines have created edges around themselves, preventing him from getting access to them.

Undoubtedly, God is now taking us through a time when everything is beyond imagination. God is exposing more to us so that there won't be any more secrets. We are now embarking on personal inventories so that we can get rid of anything that does not represent God or reflect our reality and nature in him.

Standing Against the Purpose of God

Many people believe that human beings can change God's actions. They want to control everything the Lord does instead of aligning themselves to him by faith. People are asking too many questions about everything the Lord is doing and have yet to understand that God does anything that pleases him.

While God is increasing us, science and medicine are trying to stand against it. We have not learned to keep ourselves from interfering with what the Lord is working out. We are like clay in the hands of the Potter; and God, our most trusted Potter, molds us into the shape that best fits him and us.

God gives us enough time to align ourselves with what he is doing and not stand against what he is working out. Witchcraft, and other ungodly supernatural manifestations are not the work of God; but shamefully, they have found their way into the church.

Suppose you want to control your life, to oversee everything for yourself. By deciding to do what you will and won't, you are automatically limiting the flow of God in your life.

Little Foxes That Spoil the Vine

First, we must understand that God is the vinedresser, and that Jesus is the vine, while we are the branches. God desires that all the things attached to the vine are holy and sanctified, both in their thoughts and deeds. They are made righteous by continuing to trust the Lord through faith. With faith, they can surmount every negative thought that speaks against the true character of God.

The Bible says that the word cleanses. That means when a man continues to hear the truth of God's Word and abides by them, such a man is made holy; but when a man refuses to do the same, he will begin to entertain foxes that destroy the vine (Ephesians 5:26).

For instance, the New Age ideals are stripping the church of its values, and many believers have yet to realize this. Today, the church is producing more believers who have no regard for the need for holiness, forgetting that the apostle Paul warned us, through his letter to the Galatian church, to be wary of such errors (Gal 5:13). Because of these waves of doctrine, we have more men dealing with sins that are not pronounced and confessed, which has hindered their spiritual exercise of pruning and divine assignment.

In the context of the Scriptures, foxes are *hidden* sins that may look trivial. Most of the time, they don't involve actions. They exist in the believer's mind and heart. But these sins hinder the move of God in our lives. So, the branch must be completely pruned of every little fox so that the body can be a peaceful haven where the vinedresser can dwell at will (Song of Sol 2:15).

One of the things the Lord is doing at this present time as a Master Vinedresser is the pruning of church tradition and values from the infiltration of New Age doctrines. This is necessary at this moment because it is now difficult to know those who are following God with their sincere devotion and love from those who are following the traditions of men. Men are now trying to do things according to the flesh rather than holding on to God for strength and enablement. The truth is that when the Lord is done with us, we will all see how far we have been from the true agenda and purpose he has designed for us.

Before I wrote this book, I questioned a lot of believers just to sample their opinions about how they have been fairing, especially coping with the New Age philosophies. The truth is that we have been taken farther away than expected in our walk with God. Today, many Christians have searched for voodoo and other supernatural means, all because they could not wait or trust God for their needs. Their actions have shown a lack of patience and trust. They don't see the need to be patient with what the Lord is doing with them, but they would rather move with trends.

We must not be misled, especially now, even though I was almost a casualty of this. We can't afford to be caught in the web of ignorance concerning what the Lord is doing at this time and found in the shrines and tents of sorcery. He wants us to submit ourselves wholly to him and give him all of us so he can give us all of himself.

One thing I have come to realize is that God's pruning process is not always pleasant. Take, for example, the illustration I used at the beginning of this chapter, Brian loves flowers so much. He discovers that the beauty has been distorted because of the presence of an unwanted branch that sprouted up on it. The gardener knew the best way to get rid of that and did exactly what should be done. Brian wasn't expecting him to go that far, but that was what needed to be done. To Brian, it didn't seem like the flowers needed to lose almost all their branches to gain beauty and freedom, but that pruning of everything is what brings beauty.

When God is pruning us, it is at the end of this process that we become beautiful. So, if we open up to God and give him the go-ahead in matters concerning our lives, he proves his power. We are now in an age and time when we are too quick to make decisions. We fail to carry him along as we plan our lives, and later, we become bitter and frustrated when negative things happen.

The truth is that we can't blame God because we never allowed him to lead our lives in the best way possible. One thing we must learn to do at this crucial time is to discern what the Lord is doing and what he is not doing. That understanding is essential in keeping our minds and hearts safe from deception. It is no longer news that the devil is busy instigating all sorts of tricks and cunning devices to get Christians off the path. He does this by introducing what looks like what we want, but if we can be sensitive and alert in the Spirit, we would understand that it is the devil at work.

So, as it is said, sorcery, witchcraft, and all forms of wicked acts are not from God. If we are going through warfare and it looks like everything will end soon, understand that God has a plan, and by faith, we subscribe to it rather than seek to get liberated by sorcerous means. It is common for people who are going through bitterness to do many things to hurt whoever they believe offended them. But as believers, we should understand that jealousy, unforgiveness, disappointment, and depression should not be found in us. Your duty is to pray that anyone who is doing any of these should repent and have a change of heart. So, we must keep repenting for things that may creep into our spirits and take hold of us.

As believers, we should pick out things in our lives that do not match God's Word. That's what pruning is all about. We need to emphasize again that God is still in the business of pruning man so that we become useful vessels in his hands. He wants to use vessels that have been sanctified and purified, people whose thoughts are pure and whose motives are right, men whose devotion is tilted toward him and him alone. Such men must pass through the refining fire where everything that doesn't look like God is burned away.

Now, we are in a time when people's desires and passions for God are waxing cold. The Bible says that Jesus is coming for the church, certainly not a church that is not prepared. The truth is that most churches are not prepared for the bridegroom's coming.

They are only teaching men how to become prosperous and command abundant wealth. Many pulpits have become platforms where business ideas and other irrelevant matters are discussed, and messages that can prepare men's hearts for the coming of Christ are now relatively scarce.

Cutting Down Every Weight

In Hebrews 12:1–2, the Bible states that there is a cloud of witnesses acting as spectators for the race we run. What that means is that there are godly people who inspired godly examples by the faith life they lived while on earth and are now in heaven, watching us. We should decide to replicate this behavior.

When we build a consciousness that people are cheering for us and observing how we are running the race, we will be more focused and intentional about living the life of faith.

Have you come to realize that as far as living the life of faith is concerned, we do not have any excuses? There are many people, millions of believers, who have passed through similar challenges and yet did not err from the faith. They did not allow the worries of the present age to drag them off track. They rejoice even in the face of suffering and trials. These are the people to whom we are accountable. The reason is that they, too, had similar excuses to give in, but they never did. They never relented; they forged ahead until they had the victory.

So, we need to examine our lives and check where alignments should be made. The faith walk with God is a race; running that race from start to finish and getting the prize entails us playing by the rules. No one runs a race with both their hands in their pockets. You cannot assure victory or run effectively with baggage. Pay attention to every word or circumstance that reduces your commitment and faith in God and get rid of negatives to enjoy the best of God.

New Waves of Doctrine

Part of the things the Lord, the Master Vinedresser, is doing even in this season is exposing the new waves of doctrine that are desecrating the agelong church values and traditions. People are now being deceived into believing many things that water down the effect of faith in God in their lives. People have not realized that this is what Apostle Paul spoke about in Ephesians 4:14, which says, "so that we may no longer be children, tossed to and fro by the waves and carried about by every wind of doctrine, by human cunning, by craftiness in deceitful schemes." Many have not come to realize that God desires that we should know the truth and refute anything (teaching) that can sway us away from it. Paul said we are yet children when we are tossed back and forth by this doctrine of glory. Well, it's nothing bad, but we must prune ourselves of the excesses that hinder us from holding on to the church values and standards that we have held onto for years.

One question I ask people is, "What is the purpose of gaining knowledge that reduces our commitment to God?"

A person who was once fervent in the Spirit suddenly becomes cold as soon as he gains strange knowledge called "rhema" because he believes that his fervency in the Spirit no longer moves God. On the other hand, the spoken Word of God to a person should make them more committed. What is the purpose of knowledge that fights everything the Lord is working out in our lives? God is beyond what a man can figure out. We just need to align with whatever he is doing by faith rather than attempting to change it.

Know God Beyond Philosophies

Over time, I have come to discover that the greatest mistake man has ever made was attempting to find or reduce God to someone who is in books or someone whose ways can be explained using man's knowledge. God is beyond that.

"For as the heavens are higher than the earth, so are my ways higher than your ways and my thoughts than your thoughts." (Is 55:9).

His thoughts are past figuring out. It is He that has made us and not the other way around.

Dependence on God's Strength, Not Voodoo, Hoodoo, or Shrines.

Because we have distanced ourselves from God, it has now become difficult to experience him supernaturally. And because of that, we tend to depend on our strength and wits for what we need. We have come to a time when God is no longer enough for us. We have begun to seek ways that we can obtain answers for both our natural and supernatural needs. God is ever ready and willing if we would only bring God into our lives.

Because of the fear of the unknown, most Christians have scattered the plans of God for their lives. They have allowed the worries and pain they are feeling at the moment to make them forget the promise of the Lord, which says, "Cast your burden on the LORD, and he will sustain you; he will never permit the righteous to be moved." (Ps 55:22). Whatever we might be going through, we should never lose our faith by refusing to continue acting on his words. We should take our problems to the Lord and believe that he will strengthen and keep us.

Of course, today, we still have believers who see nothing bad or unscriptural with depending on black magic, witch doctors, and other forms of manipulation to obtain their desires. "For by professing it some have swerved from the faith." (1 Tim 6:21a). They are using supernatural things for natural gains, reducing the manifestations of God's power in their lives.

They are looking for acceptance and relevance, and in their attempt to do so, they suppress the truth of God's Word. They make the Bible suit what they want to communicate. These people are everywhere in the church today. They gather people and begin teaching them everything that has ever watered down the agelong sacred values of the church.

These teachings promote self-reliance. They elevate the knowledge and strength of man more than the knowledge of God. God is still the ultimate master planner, and his wisdom has not gone away and will never go into extinction. Hold on to it and enjoy the fulfillment that is waiting for those who lean on him for everything they need.

Faith Is the Truth

If you are longing for the truth, it is vital for you to know that the actual nature of God is that of faith. That is why anyone who wants to come to him should know that without faith it is impossible to please him. For whoever would draw near to God must believe that he exists and that he rewards those who seek him (Heb 11:6). That verse started by telling us that *without faith, it is impossible to please Him.* So, there are two vital things here. First, pleasing God comes from faith; and second, faith produces a reward. We can say that those who have known faith in the truth about God are eligible for rewards. Do not look to receive rewards though; just be grateful to receive them.

With God, there is a reward system. When you know the truth, the Bible says it will make you free. That is one of the rewards. When a man does not know God enough, he may not enjoy the blessed assurance (confidence or faith) in him.

Everything against faith is against the truth, and anything against the truth is against God. You cannot claim to know the truth and not have faith, and you can't have faith and not have God.

The reason why many people are struggling today is that they have left the faith part out, and without faith, everything else is fruitless.

Right Positioning for Pruning

God is opening our minds currently, allowing us to retrace our steps and do what is needed. He wants us to be zealous and diligent with the assignment he committed into our hands. And the good news is he is ready to cut off every unnecessary weight and sin that limits the flow of his power. Our duty as man is to rightly position ourselves for God to use us to fulfill his will. We should not fight against it by trying to control it using our carnal knowledge. God is all-knowing. We must believe that he won't give us anything harmful. God is working everything together for our good as the Good Shepherd and Gardener does (Rom 8:28).

Faith and Spiritual Warfare

I would venture to say that spiritual warfare is negative energy that the enemy uses to make us Christians stop doing things that are unbecoming or sinful of a Christian. They can also use this energy to push you into positive actions. The enemy can and will use close relatives, members of your community, and even church members to do his bidding. I must admit that the whole thing left me in a bit of a quandary until I began to listen to individual perspectives on the subject. Lately, this has been a hot topic in the Christian community. Every pastor who has ever graced my television set on Sunday morning seems to have been given the charge of leading us through spiritual warfare. The following are generally what happens during the process:

1. We will lose friends and some family members-they will hurt and then abandon us but then we come to find out that it was God separating us, by pruning.
2. God shows us our enemies and they show us all their colors.

3. We are tormented more, and this is when we should begin reestablishing ourselves.
4. We will be told lies mixed with truth. Is this retribution for a wrong I have done or is it God wanting me, or a mixture of both. We must believe that it is God no matter what the enemy says, or you might find yourself in very deep despair. I cannot begin to tell you how important it is to draw near to God because deep despair is only a small description of the pain and how much you will want to give up.
5. We must focus on our goals, both spiritual and personal and how we are going to accomplish them with God leading the way.
6. We must always remember that we never want Him to say that he never knew us so we must trust him in every aspect of our lives-He will prove to you that only in Him you can depend-The Relationship is what counts.
7. The Bible is one way God communicates with us. This is why it is called the Living Word. He will make known what everything means while you are reading it. He will tell us what we can get from what we are reading. Wherever you start in the Bible, he will show you something there for you and your situation. Of course, you can still go to the sections marked for their particular purpose, but God is amazing, and he will meet you wherever you are. That last sentence has many meanings as well. The point is there is none like him and there never will be.

Why pain we ask? The Bible says that God is very near to the broken in spirit. He chooses to shake us in the middle of our adversities. At these times he will draw us closer. Some spiritual advisors will say that this pruning/warfare is to be taken as motivation to push us forward. Others will say it is to train us up for harder things that are to come. Yet there are others that say that we must share in the pain that Jesus had to suffer through. I believe that it could be all the above.

When we look at the Bible, we see so many examples of people who had to go through adversities. For example, Joseph went to jail, Daniel was in the Lion's den, the three Hebrew children were in the furnace, and I can go on. The point is that God could have done this differently by not allowing them to suffer at all, but he did not. In allowing these problems to move forth we realize that God is all we have to depend on. All these people were drawn closer to him through their suffering.

He invites us to share in the pain that his son had to endure. When I look back on it all, I realize that it is the least I can do, suffer the embarrassment, and pain that comes along with this walk. It does not compare in the least to what Jesus had to suffer through.

"The LORD is near to the brokenhearted and saves the crushed in spirit." (Ps 34:18).

It is best to choose this time wisely. We should become the best versions of ourselves as possible. The whole process can become daunting, but we must remain focused. I have often felt trapped and very depressed. It was during one of these times that I thought about the poem by Maya Angelou entitled, I know why the caged bird sings. It was in the 70's that the young ladies from my church were taken to a reading from this book by Ms. Angelou in person.

She looked confident and poised as she spoke the words that I will never forget. The caged bird can dream of doing the things that the free bird can. It is imagined that the caged bird sings of freedom. These are the thoughts that we often think about during the time of our suffering. We have all thought unimaginable thoughts during these times. God wants us to draw near to him and tell him about all our problems. Yes. He already knows but, we must think in terms of relationship. Remember, that if we don't have a relationship with him, what would he have to say to us on that great gettin' up morning?

His ways are so much more advanced than our own that we have no idea what his entire plan is. This is why it is very important to depend on your faith in God and in his love for us. If I told you that God can make plans for us years in advance and all of it can fall into place, what would you say? Don't say anything just have faith.

God often reminds me that he is still with me during my suffering. In the very beginning, I was a total mess, about at the end of my rope when suddenly my head turned toward the TV. The lady said, "I know that God is always with me." Saints, let me tell you that the show that was 'just on' was called A Haunting. When I finally decided to look at it to take my mind off my woes, this is what happened. I also work in the Healthcare field. We can have five different people, from five different places in one day coming in for left foot pain. Before I was awakened, I didn't notice things like this but now I see he is speaking to me all the time. The next day it will be five people with right elbow pain. I have to stop and tell the Lord that I know you are here Father, and I recognize your power. You can do anything, even group people's injuries, because you are a God of order. I just have to smile and feel comforted. I can tell you so much more that has happened to give me comfort and know that God is all knowing and all powerful. I haven't been to Sunday school since I was a teen. Since I have been going through my trial I started back. The Sunday school lesson in July was concerning this very thing. It actually said that this is a test of our faith and that God wanted no one left behind. The comfort from this lasted for a little while and then I began to have doubts. The enemy kept telling me things like; how could you do what you did to me? This is because of what you did, and I would have doubt again and fall back into despair. Yes, just as I said in the introduction, I did make a mess of things and the enemy tells me that this is just revenge. We must know that we have a God of Justice but not torture. Again, we must use discernment and pray for this.

"Indeed, we felt that we had received the sentence of death. But that was to make us rely not on ourselves but on God who raises the dead." (2 Cor 1:9).

Of course, my constant despair leaves my family, and my church family, feeling helpless because they told me what was happening. I have come to realize that it takes more than once or twice. This is a powerful thing, this spiritual warfare. I have learned that I must feed my spirit man with praise and worship several times during the week. I can't wait for Bible study or Sunday Morning worship, or I will go into deep despair again and again. It is a constant battle with no time off for good behavior. There was once a song that said only the strong survive. Well, I am saying that this is true but who can give us strength? I am beginning to realize that my family, pastor, and church family as wonderful as they are, are only human, and yes, they will become frustrated with me at times. As I said, God wants us to know that he never gets tired and that we will always have him no matter what - the relationship. I believe that he enjoys constantly reminding us that he is there. Let me not get off track here. On another occasion of falling back into despair I found God clearly in my daily devotionals. It is 2023 but I have been drawn into going back through a devotional that was given to me by a dear cousin from 2011. On the morning of July 3rd, it read, 'I'm inviting you to share in the disgrace of Jesus.' The next morning it read, 'I am teaching you to rely on Me and not yourself.' Here are a few more to give you food for thought:

July 5th- "I will elevate you to a place of great honor."

July 6th – 'My word is exposing what needs to be cut away."

July 7th – "I will not be fair; I will show mercy." (Guthrie, 2011).

I would venture to say that God planned all this years ago. I would also like to say that most of these devotionals, i.e. abundant life,

Jesus Calling, etc. if not all of them were actually inspired by God if not written totally by his voice. It is far too much information relating to what we are going through to be coincidental. This is why we say let those who have ears to hear and eyes to see do so etc. Everything will seem coincidental until God changes you. It is then that you will hear and see just what is going on around you. You will be 'awake' finally. Not in the new age sense but in the God sense. Satan has become very bold in what his doing. He is in our faces with hate and concert theatrics, therefore; I believe that God is being more purposeful in his actions and communications. It is a war after all.

I mentioned television evangelists earlier. I have always been a fervent follower of TBN, The Word Network, Daystar etc. and will continue to be. It seems that nearly all if not all of them were going through some type of scandal during this process, just as we are. Now all of them have been called to help us get through this time. What I believe about this is that God does not waste a work that he is doing. He will use and sweep up everything in his path. He is also showing us love through forgiveness. What I am saying is that everyone will gain something from the process, not just us but the teachers who have been given these messages as well. Even the local pastors are gaining what they need. There is no one who is exempt from what God is doing in this hour.

Since God has taken a mighty stand, he has his prophets as well as the evangelists working to help us. We must be careful because there are piranhas out there seeking who they can destroy for various reasons. This is another area where we must use discernment. Ask God to help us in this area so that we are not taken in by the enemy.

"Resist him, firm in your faith, knowing that the same kinds of suffering are being experienced by your brotherhood throughout the world." 1 Peter 5:91

Although it feels as if the wait will be over maybe as soon as tomorrow, it isn't up to us, and we still have no way of knowing the exact day or hour that our Lord will come for his children. In this book, I encourage whoever has ears to hear that they must continuously work out their faith. It will take our obedience to be able to stand in these last days. Yes, I'm saying that we are living in the last days and that every house should be in order. We can't afford to miss out on anything that the Lord is saying to us at this time. This is the most important reason that we are in spiritual warfare. Again, the Father does not want any of his children left behind. He wants to help us get it right. In fact, most of this book has been about spiritual warfare. We are pruned and tried in the fire. Don't get discouraged if you mess up, he just wants you to do it again until you get it right but, try hard to get it right. Our God is a loving God, regardless of what it looks like around us, we must keep our focus on Him.

I encourage all to read their Bibles and stay on top of true current events. I emphasize the word true because there is news and then there is news that is more informative. Because the news has been less and less informative concerning very important events it has led me to seek God's word even more. I am looking to it as a guide to events that are about to take place. In case you have not been aware, the events of the Bible are unfolding right now. It leads me to watch television evangelists to gather knowledge. All around the nation everyone is speaking the same language, giving the same message, and listening to the same woes. There seems to be one wave among the saints currently. As I mentioned earlier, we must all prepare, for God's return like never before. God wants us all to be ready for his return and not be caught off guard like the five virgins described in the Bible. While five were smart and kept oil in their lamps and extra oil in flasks, the other five were not so smart. The latter did not and when the bridegroom came for them, they were not ready. Although they later tried to be let into the festivities, the answer from within was no, I do not know you. Does that sound familiar? The Lord says in Matthew 7:21 "'Not everyone who says to me, 'Lord, Lord,' will enter the kingdom of heaven, but the one who does the will of my Father who is in heaven.'" They will say they prophesied in His name and healed in his name, and he will say I never knew you. What I'm saying is that we must be wise at this time. Learn about the Lord, from the Lord (His living word). The Lord wants those who are seeking him to commune with like-minded people, therefore it is good to attend church. Iron sharpens iron is a good way to look at it.

You must be saying by now that this is frightening information that I'm giving you. You would be correct in this assumption. I am trying to scare the hell right out of you. This is how much I believe in you and how much I know the Lord doesn't want you to miss out on Him. You don't want the constant fire of hell when all you had to do was follow his word. There should be no reason to doubt any of it. Nothing about it tells you to do anything that is wrong. It is quite the opposite, which is right.

Although these times are hard, we can take solace in his gift of peace. "Peace I leave with you; my peace I give to you. Not as the world gives do I give to you. Let not your hearts be troubled, neither let them be afraid." (John 14:27).

While there is no getting around the times that we are living in, we notice not-so-subtle other tones in the atmosphere. We are waiting and watching and becoming restless. All around us people are encouraging us to wait on the Lord. Why wait? It is time that we are obedient is why. Look at what was done for us. After all, did Jesus not pay the ultimate redemptive price for us? So, while we are busy creating better versions of ourselves, time continues to move forward and waiting seems to make us even more cognizant of the time.

While we worry, becoming anxious and sometimes insulant about how slowly things are moving, won't help our situation at all. Our negative impulses or attitudes cannot stop the seconds from ticking by nor the minutes or hours from doing their perspective jobs. We are indeed at square one, where we are waiting on the Lord. And after you have done your inner makeover, i.e. helping the poor, being kind, etc. what then? Having done all we can, we can then stand and try to enjoy the rest of our lives, while we wait. Learn how to laugh and dream again. When we can laugh at ourselves and are not so serious, this is an accomplishment alone. We should praise the Lord while we wait because we know that he is there. "Yet you are holy, enthroned on the praises of Israel." (Ps 22:3). I have learned to take this verse a step further. Since I know he is there when I praise, I praise often.

Key Takeaways

- God is all-knowing, a vinedresser whose work is to prune us so that we can be aligned with what he is doing.

- Our work as humans is not to fight or try to control the work of God through science, medicine, technology, and other means.

- We must get rid of our every weight, little foxes, and unbelief that is limiting the influence of God.

Chapter 3

FAITH WALK

Have you ever wondered why it seems difficult to hear God in this Internet-driven society? Are you wondering why there has been an increase in the number of false prophets in these last days?

Many people are trying to access the sacred secrets of heaven and trying to find out what the Lord is doing even now. People are trying to travel into the heavens and bring messages for self-aggrandizement by the methods God has forbidden. But God desires that we pray every time and never cease. He wants us to pray and never to faint because "if you faint in the day of adversity, your strength is small." (Prov 24:10).

God's will is simple—to put him first. He wants man to acknowledge him in all his ways so that he can guide and protect him in his ways. Before doing anything, God wants us to receive instruction from him and act accordingly. Before we start our daily tasks, he wants us to seek direction. The truth is the Lord is ever willing to direct and inspire us on the correct path to follow. There is a limit to what we can do or achieve if we remove God from the equation. Today, we have men who want you to believe that you can achieve everything all by yourself, relying on your wits and strength; but that's not the agenda of God for his children.

God created everyone with what is known as "the dependency tendency." That means that every man is created with the need for God. Don't play the route of self-deception by thinking that everything you need can be made possible through science and technology. Believers who have that belief can tell you how much they suffer. That means you are doing everything for yourself without God's help or assistance. This kind of thinking tends to end in utter frustration.

God knows how limited and fragile we are. He knows we can't do it all alone. But he wants you to invite him so he can perform the unusual. He wants you to be filled with faith so everything can be made possible. The Bible says, "and blessed is she who believed that there would be a fulfillment of what was spoken to her from the Lord" (Luke 1:45). I have seen many people misused by the devil because they believed that God had given them all there was to live a fulfilled life. These people don't pray for God's help. They don't pray for divine intervention and support; they just believe that God has done his part, and the rest is left in their hands to control. Well, that seems cool and logical, but it is devoid of faith.

The ways of the Lord most often do not make sense to us. It is against technology and science and can't be explained through tradition or philosophy. It is not an understatement to say that the achievement of modern science undermines faith. Most interviews with tech gurus or scientists end with them stating that they or either agnostic or atheist and that they credit themselves for their successes.

Modern science and technology plus philosophy would have us see life and everything from their end; but there seems to be nothing they will do as far as God's power, existence, and creativity are concerned. We should enjoy what God has prepared for us.

How good would things be if men could believe in God as they do in science and medicine? We have so much trust that healing is found in science and medicine; that is why our minds go there whenever we have challenges. The truth is when someone is ill, the first place the mind of an average believer will go is the hospital or pharmacy. We have allowed science to define life and everything in it for us, and that has limited the flow of God's power.

Let's get a bit personal. Some years ago, I lost my aunt. She had been sick for a while, and we tried everything we could to help her. We thought that western medicine could cure her illness. She lost her battle for life in this world. She was a faith-driven woman, and the period between the day the doctors told her of the cancer and the day she died was fourteen years. They were not bedridden years but happy and fruitful years. God gave her fourteen years to be happy on this earth with us before he claimed her.

On the verge of losing yet another loved one, we summoned the courage to believe in God for the miraculous. Obviously, we came to the end of our wits and power. My grandmother was diagnosed with cancer. The period between the time that she was diagnosed with cancer and the time that she died was twenty years. You can't tell me what God can't do.

We can't say who will be healed or when; we need only to have faith.

What did I learn? God is a constant factor.

He is always willing to help our weaknesses if only we can rely on him and give him first place in our hearts. We must learn to create a consciousness that God loves us too much to forget us in our sorrows and tribulations. He wants us to have a perfect relationship with him so much that we can believe him for anything we need.

The truth is our minds have been trained to be on the carnal and vain things of this world. We only want to believe what we see and what we hear. We are quick to judge everything using our senses and knowledge, but when God's agenda comes into perspective, we will begin to reason or see things the way he does. Maybe until then can we believe that everything is possible once we put our trust and hope in God.

What we need to understand is, for God, nothing is impossible. That also goes for us. He wants us to rise above vain or carnal fixations to a place where we can accurately discern the mind and purpose of God from his perspective. He wants us to key into his plan using our *sixth sense*. What do I mean by this statement? Our faith, of course. Today, everyone wants results. We all want to talk to God by every means, but we are not going through the right channel. We want to access God from the realm of carnality, where God is unlikely to be found.

Because of our passion for supernatural results, the spirits of carnality, witchcraft, and other vices of the devil have taken center stage. But God has given us an anchor—his Word. He said we should try every spirit and ensure we disregard any utterances that the Holy Spirit does not sponsor. Such spirits are deceptive and antichrist. "Beloved, do not believe every spirit, but test the spirits to see whether they are from God, for many false prophets have gone out into the world" (1 John 4:1).

They produce results that are temporary and flesh edifying. The Holy Spirit produces results that edify men's souls and glorify God.

I think the major issue of why it seems that hearing God and believing him for everything is difficult is that most people have not attuned themselves to hear the voice of God. Some people are so trained to believe what they see rather than recognizing the *still small voice* that speaks from within them or when we read the Bible. That voice inspires and directs us in our walk with God. But it does not force his will on us. He does not forcefully compel us to obey; he wants us to surrender to his will and act by faith. Until you realize that you need him and cry out to him just like a baby would cry to his mother to be fed, God may not move.

Our Faith Releases the Power of God

The woman with the issue of blood in the Bible had tried many things to try and cure her illness. Many physicians had come to help her without success. As soon as the woman saw Jesus, she recognized him and released her faith. Her faith attracted the power of God where Science had failed her. Physicians came to the end of their knowledge. Medicinal herbs lost their potency in her case. But God stepped in, and the situation changed.

As we walk with God in faith, we should keep listening to his voice as he instructs us. There is no shortcut to the supernatural. It is either obedience or disobedience. We obey by believing his words. But we can't believe words that we do not read. The sermon we hear in the pulpit on Sundays and those snippets we read online are not enough for our faith walk. We must be intentional about studying the Word for ourselves. It is the Word that we read and digest that becomes what we function with.

Paul knew the importance of the Word. That was why he instructed Timothy to study to show that he was approved as a workman and needed not be ashamed but rightly dividing the Word of truth (2 Tim 2:15). The Word of God can wrongly be divided or misinterpreted if it falls into the hands of ignorant or unlearned men, men who lack a basic understanding of the principles of Bible interpretation.

In Luke 4, the Bible states that Jesus was tempted in the wilderness. What amazed me was the responses of Jesus to those tempting words. Satan, who understood the basic needs of Jesus at that time, commanded him to do certain things contrary to the purpose of God; but Jesus objected. The rejection of such enticing offers could only come from the mind that houses the knowledge of God's word. If we had been in Jesus's place, would we have fallen for the same temptations?

We believe that if we don't eat healthy food, we will not gain the needed nutrients for our bodies to function properly. The same goes for the edification and building of our spiritual edifice too. If we refuse to believe God's word for it every moment, the word might not be able to work for us when we need it the most.

One thing I have learned about God is that he is pleased when we nourish our spirits. And I think I know why. It is easier for God to instruct and direct a more informed heart than an uninformed one. God delights in seeing men who walk out his word. God knows that when he instructs an informed heart, carrying out his will is not hard. I once believed that science was more consistent with results than faith was until God proved me wrong. I thought everything was possible with science. When we are sick, we go to the hospital, the doctor prescribes drugs, we use them, and we are healthy again. When we get to a dark place where our visibility is blurred, we just turn on a light. When we want to travel to a place, we simply get into our car and drive off. No stress. We don't need faith or prayer to get that done. In the same vein, some people would argue on why we need God for healing when a doctor can prescribe drugs. They would argue that we should know how to make ships rather than walk on the sea like Jesus. I would argue that God would like nothing more than to be a part of their lives and for them to see that he is real.

Years ago, many philosophers championed campaigns for individualism and secularism. This coincided with scientific inventions and advancements that changed the way people perceived God. We have been made to see everything logically and critically from the point of human perspective and scientific analysis. But that is not an exercise backed up by faith.

Faith begins where science and logical sense end. When we see the results and can attest to the viability of something, we tend not to believe God for it. It is better if you realize that science and technology don't have all the answers to human problems. *After all, faith is beyond solving all human problems; it is our walk with God that is the answer.* Our God is unseen, yet he exists. Just as we can't see air but can't deny its significant presence, so it is with God.

The truth is there are natural realities, and there are also spiritual realities. Both realms operate on principles. Certain things have been scientifically proven to be genuine because they have passed through several scientific observations. For example, scientists believe everything we can see, feel, and touch exists. Science tries to define everything God created using its own words and rules. Yet it fails to accept that there is a person in charge of everything we see. This is also applicable to spiritual reality. In the spiritual realms, some realities are real, and they can't be explained using human or scientific knowledge.

Let's start with the plan of God for salvation. The Bible records in 1 Corinthians 2:9, "But, as it is written, 'What no eye has seen, nor ear heard, nor the heart of man imagined, what God has prepared for those who love him.'" That verse affirms that no man has seen or known the plan. The simple truth is it was not meant to be revealed to man until the time appointed by the Father. Remember, many verses of the Scriptures affirm that the plan has been from the foundation of the world. But it can't be known or searched out by man. Even when the plan was revealed to men, they rejected it.

The Scriptures say in 1 Corinthians 1:22, "For Jews demand signs and Greeks seek wisdom," That's the same with faith. Scientists, philosophers, and other knowledgeable men after the flesh are looking for ways to explain God through what they know. But God can only be seen and explained by faith.

The apostle Paul further asked, "where is the one who is wise? Where is the scribe? Where is the debater of this age? Has not God made foolish the wisdom of the world?" and "For the foolishness of God is wiser than men, and the weakness of God is stronger than men." (1 Cor 1:20, 25). God primarily designed faith as a means of access to him. So, faith *is intentional.* It comes through hearing the truth of God's words and acting accordingly. God chose the *faith walk* as the only way to walk with him. The Bible says, "by faith, Enoch walked with God; he was pleased and was kept from dying" (Heb 11:5). Although Abraham was old and had an aged body, he hoped for another reality rather than the weaknesses of his body. Faith exposes our weaknesses and allows us to receive supernatural help. We keep producing results that will wow our generations. If we acknowledge that there is a higher reality that only God can make possible, the generations will notice.

The faith walk produces blessings, the ones that last forever. Remember, God is as powerful as the man that walks by faith and not by sight (2 Cor 5:7).

Key Takeaways

- Hearing God and walking in his ways has become difficult in this Internet-driven age because we tend to believe what we see or hear or feel more than the unseen reality of God that can only be accessed through and by faith.

- Modern science and technology have limited results that cannot stand the test of time without distortion.

- Faith is beyond solving all human problems; it is a walk with God.

- Our faith releases the power of God.

- God shows his power when man walks by faith and not by sight.

Chapter 4

FAITH IN THE NEW AGE

Let's start with the inspiring story of Doreen Virtue, which she revealed through an article published recently. According to her, she had written many courses and books that brought her fame and fortune, promoting New Age practices until she saw the true light of God and embraced it.

As recent as some five years back, she was the world's top-selling New Age author. During that period, she enjoyed a very lucrative lifestyle. She lived on a ranch of about fifty acres in Hawaii. During this period, she would stay in penthouse hotels and rub elbows with prominent people. Her publisher treated her like a rock star, flying her and her husband on first-class tickets worldwide.

Yet despite living this luxurious life and affluence, she hardly knew peace. Despite her New Age successes, there were answers she was never able to find.

She grew up in the Church of Christian Science, although her parents made her believe that they were Christians. Virtue was taught to neglect the seemingly negative parts of the Bible, such as the crucifixion of Jesus and the fall of humanity. This continued for so long that when she studied the Scriptures, she cherry-picked verses or interpreted them out of context. So, she opened her heart to the devil's deception.

Virtue went to Chapman University in California, earned degrees, and became a professional therapist. While at the university, Doreen Virtue found a literary agent and started writing self-help books for prominent publishers. This paved the way for her to speak and appear at conferences and radio and television, where she predominantly inspired and taught people about the gospel of self-help. After a while, she met a New Age publisher who offered to convert her psychology dissertation into a self-help book. She agreed, and that began to indoctrinate her into Christian Science beliefs. Doreen soon became a regular speaker with a group of New Age teachers who traveled to conventions both far and near.

During breaks from the podium, she would visit the various New Age kiosks. She was intrigued by the crystals and other wares they showcased and their advanced healing. It was from these vendors she learned more about practices and New Age beliefs.

During her twenty years of being a New Age teacher, she taught with other best-selling authors. Her agenda, and that of other proponents, was to promote techniques like positive affirmations and vision boards. She was teaching people to believe that their words can create their reality. Virtue revealed how she twisted all the statements of Jesus to suggest that God would give anyone what they say or believe. And all the while, she held up her fame and wealth as evidence that her principles and beliefs were accurate and effective.

Yet despite all these achievements and successes, all her life and that of other New Age teachers were marred with all sorts of unscriptural activities. Divorces and addictions were common happenings in their lives. The highest number of sold workshops, cheering fans, standing ovations, and connections attached to her name gave her a very swollen ego. She believed that every thought and inspiration she got came from God or his holy angels. Surprisingly, throughout this period, she was still convinced that she was a Christian but an open-minded

Christian who was superior to all narrow-minded followers whose devotion and love was to Jesus only. For her, Jesus operated as a "spirit guide" who, like a superior master, helped her make wishes come true. She was practically a student of world religions. She had a necklace with symbols of all the major faiths. She believed in harmonizing all religions; according to her, all paths led to heaven, and all faiths worship the same God. According to her story, neither she nor other New Age proponents ever pointed to the real Jesus Christ. She said she never told people to read their Bibles. Instead, they encouraged people to pursue their inclinations, making them more materialistic and covetous.

If you are not familiar with Doreen Virtue's story, you probably need to understand this New Age movement that advances the principles of self-spirituality with a focus on personal development, connection, evolution, and deep relation with the universe. This movement emphasized that all paths lead to heaven. You don't have to become a Christian to be sure you are going to heaven; this concept promotes and defines spirituality apart from Christ. Finally, this movement is about getting people to believe that they can achieve anything they desire just by connecting to their maker and drawing the inspiration needed for success.

This is what many people are confessing and professing to in this present day, and it has become a new normal even in the church of God. Many people have shifted their focus and have lost their first love because of their passion for fame and relevance. They are taught to believe that Jesus is just a spirit guide, not a savior, not a ticket to heaven, but someone who can inspire man with needed tools to achieve anything man's soul desires.

One thing evident from Doreen Virtue's confession is that New Age teachers place a premium on actualizing desire and personal dreams using their intellect and wits. They make people believe that anything is achievable if they can think about it. So, all a man needs to succeed in life is just a desire and work toward it, and with much dedication, they will definitely meet their goals with or without God. Doesn't that negate faith?

That seems to reduce the potency of faith and makes believing in God irrelevant. But one thing that is usually common among these people is that they lose touch with God. Despite their wealth accumulation and influence, this space is always in the heart. They desire a true God, and until they realize the need to retrace their steps, they have no peace.

One of the things I have noticed about New Age teachers is that they are usually ministry people, meaning that they started out as ministers in prominent assemblies, ministering for Jesus and compelling the hearts of men to follow him. But after a while, the quest for fame and prominence drew them away from the faith into what the apostle Paul called *another gospel.* New Age theories are high-sounding. They are compelling, but they seem to lose relevance because someone who gives sustainability to every message and belief is missing.

While most Christians nowadays claim they believe in God of the Bible, many still hold onto one or more of the fundamental principles of the New Ager—astrology, psychics, reincarnation, and the presence of spiritual powers that are in objects such as hills, water, mountains, or trees. Even though some of these beliefs outrightly contradict the truth the Bible teaches, most of them have subtly trickled into the church.

Plausibly even more dangerous is the self-actualization and love ideology that is being taught to many Christians today and is regarded as the truth. What this means is, at first glance, you almost believe that these beliefs resonate with the truth contained in the Bible until you carefully observe them.

Through close observation, you will see that these beliefs are founded upon the principles of New Agers rather than what the Bible really teaches.

Though the Bible affirms that every believer has intrinsic value because they are made in the nature and image of God, the same Bible quickly affirms that without God, we can do nothing. The Bible says, "abide in me, and I in you. As the branch cannot bear fruit by itself, unless it abides in the vine, neither can you, unless you abide in me." (John 15:4).

With that Bible reference and many others, the position of God concerning believers' actualization of purpose and dreams is evident. When Christ is removed from the picture, faith is eliminated from the scene; and when that happens, carnality sets in. Everything becomes too natural to be true.

According to Steven Bancarz, a former New Ager and now a Christian apologist, Satan is trying his best to deceive people with the lie he started many years ago, nothing new but the one he started in Genesis 3. You know, "you will be like God." He is making everyone feel as if they don't need God and have all they need to act and produce the same result as God. But when these lies entangle us, we are captured and tempted to believe that life is simply about bettering our social standing or character and that we can get everything from life through mindfulness, meditation, the positive affirmations mindset, and self-reliance.

You should beware. This is certainly not the gospel Jesus called us into. The goal of Christ is to make us like himself, to help our infirmities by strengthening us so we will not be shortchanged. And to do this, faith must be activated. We must be deliberate with our walk of faith. This has to do with denying self, taking up our crosses, and following him as he leads the way. God knows how limited and futile human efforts can be. He knows how vulnerable we are without his assistance. He knows that there is always a vacuum in the mind of every person that only he can fill; that is why he commanded us to surrender all to him so he can take us through the journey and help us when we don't believe that we can go on.

The faith life is not a life of self-actualization but rather a life of self-denial, a life that you need to die to yourself so that the glory of God can manifest mightily. This does not mean we don't have value; rather, there is nothing good in us that we can do without God since every man is great with the greatest desire to find satisfaction in God.

When you are not aligning with the purpose and plan of God for your life, you will always have the feeling that something is missing, especially when you have not yielded and have moved away from the faith. Fulfilling his desires and pleasure is what gives us joy. Only through Jesus Christ and his finished work on the cross can we bring to the perfection and purpose that which the Lord has destined for us.

Another thing that makes New Age beliefs questionable is that they do not regard the place of Christ as the ultimate and only access and source of supernatural power. Jesus said, "I am the way, and the truth, and the life. No one comes to the Father except through me." (John 14:6). This is a profound truth that many religious leaders are still contending with today. None of the other religious leaders who have lived and died, and some whose sepulchers are still with us today, made that statement. In fact, many of them couldn't assure their followers that they were going to make it to heaven. And if their eternity was not certain, it is dangerous to affirm that their followers will make it either. Some even frankly told them to go in search of the truth.

For someone to believe that there are other ways to access the heaven apart from Jesus shows that the person has not come into the reality of the truth that the Bible teaches even though they are Christians. If one understands the nature and character of God, as explained in the Bible, they know that God is not someone who can be accessed through various other means.

Faith vs. New Age: The Missing Link

If you have not studied the New Age philosophies very well, you may think that Christianity and the New Age share similar or the same views. Many Christians have been deceived into thinking that way. They think God's agenda for man after salvation is for man to begin to control everything God created for his own good and desire. But after carefully observing these beliefs, they came out to understand that New Age beliefs are entirely different from the plan of God for man.

As Christians, we are saved through grace, and that grace is powered by faith in the finished work of Christ. But we don't stop there. We take it a step further in knowing God and revealing him in all our dealings on earth. After we receive him as our Lord and Savior, what actually happens is that from that moment, God begins to exert his leadership and authority through us. We become a vessel that communicates God's agenda and purpose. But for us to actively play this role, we must believe and constantly act in faith.

We can say that faith is the missing link between true Christianity and New Age beliefs. While faith emphasizes the need to rely on supernatural help and effort, New Age beliefs emphasize self-actualization. And the Bible affirms that without faith, no one can please the Lord.

Faith Produces Edification, While New Agers Bring Inspiration

If you listen closely to a New Ager, you might conclude that all your problems are gone. Sweet words, glowing speech, and compelling utterances might make you think you have been fooling yourself by acting in faith. But when you check deeply, you will realize there is fluff when there should be truth. They have well-arranged words, rhymes, and quotes that can inspire you. As soon as you hear those words, you feel like you are in third heaven. Nothing is difficult. You want to try everything. You may take steps to achieve everything your soul desires as they have told you, but after a while, you understand that there is more to it than inspiration.

As believers, the messages we listen to, the sermons we hear, and the Christian books we read should *end up* edifying our spirit man. They should draw us closer to the person of Jesus and not take us farther away from him. If you were a 5 on a scale of 1 to 5 in your relationship before you listened to or read them, they should fuel up your passion for more of him.

Some believers today seem to have erred. The Bible says such people can't endure sound doctrine, so they produce teachers who will teach them what they want to hear rather than what the Bible teaches. "For the time is coming when people will not endure sound teaching, but having itching ears they will accumulate for themselves teachers to suit their own passions," (2 Tim 4:3). No doubt we are now in the perilous times that the apostle Paul spoke about. We are in a season when people are promoting human philosophies against the knowledge of Christ. They are teaching this, and they take pleasure in those who believe them. But the Bible's stand on this is evident. We should cling to what is true and forget about other things that look like the truth.

As I said earlier, most New Agers are probably not unbelievers; they are likely people who have once tasted the goodness of God. They were perhaps teachers and respected individuals who held relevant and key church positions. Paul said they have the form of Godliness, but they denied the power thereof (2 Tim 3:5), just like the comment Apostle Paul gave concerning Demas. He said Demas had forsaken him, having loved this present world (2 Tim 4:10). They, too, for the sake of pleasure, wealth, and fame, left the path of righteousness and clung to the path that is alien to the faith.

Peace Unquantifiable

Here is another missing link. We should come to realize that peace can only be found in Christ. In fact, we won't know how valuable that peace is until we lose it. Nothing will seem to work. It might seem as if the world is against us.

Let's use this example: how do you usually feel when you act against the counsel of the Lord?

Don't tell me. I know. I have been there.

The peace the Scriptures describe, that surpasses all understanding, is lost. We may think that we are doing the right thing. The world may applaud us. We may get more connected to people that matter. Recommendations, awards, and such might be in abundance for us; but I'm sure there is something we can't tell people. There are some questions we need to have answered. That is the usual feeling for those who left the faith in pursuit of any self-actualization goal or agenda.

Acting in faith, even though we have yet to see results, brings joy and peace. We are just happy to be doing the will of God. We are not disturbed, and nothing terrifies us. Acting in faith is acting according to God's Word, and that is faith. When we act in faith, we are living in obedience, and one of the blessings of obedience is peace of mind. This peace is not the same as what the world can give. New Agers don't seem to have it, so they can't promise us that. It can only be accessed through and by faith in Christ.

Anytime I think of the peace we get through faith in Christ, one verse of Scripture that comes to mind is Isaiah 26:3. That verse says, "You keep him in perfect peace whose mind is stayed on you, because he trusts in you." If you consider the words of the Scripture very well, you will observe that the Bible says people whose minds have not swayed away. Those whose thoughts and imaginations are fixed on God will have peace roundabout. You won't know the value of this peace until you lose it.

In conclusion, as believers, we must not be part of the six in ten American adults who believe in New Age philosophies (Quick, 2018). We can't give our lives to Christ and still believe we can do it alone. God takes pride in helping us. He wants us to believe he is an ever-present help in times of need. Remember, he saved us. Since he has all mighty power to buy our freedom through his redeeming blood there is no mountain nor issue, he would not solve for us. Just believe and be open to receiving. I am not saying that everything you want you will get but if it is his will for your life and in his timing he will.

Key Takeaways

- The New Age movement promotes the principles of self-spirituality, focusing on personal development, connection, evolution, and deep relation with the universe.

- This movement is all about getting people to believe that they can achieve anything they desire just by connecting to their maker and drawing the inspiration needed for success.

- The Faith life is not a life of self-actualization but, rather, a life of self-denial and total belief in the help of the savior Jesus Christ.

Chapter 5

WHAT DO WE KNOW ABOUT FAITH?

Whether you were just born again, have been in the faith for years, or aren't sure you are ready for the journey yet, you've probably heard the word "faith" countless times. But you might not be sure it's such a big deal. You hear people say, "I know everything will work together for good as the Lord has planned it if I just have faith!"

You've probably also heard people say, "We know you are going through the most difficult period, but just have faith in God. Everything will be better soon." And then you wonder what it means.

Faith has to do with believing or trusting the Word of God. It is acting according to God's Word. Let's say someone is facing a difficult moment, and we ask that person to stay calm and have faith; we are telling the person to hold on and act upon God's Word concerning that matter.

In a situation where someone has nothing, and he is proclaiming he has everything in Christ, that might seem crazy to some. That's what is known as the faith approach. It is when we allow our actions to correspond with what is written in the Bible for us.

Today, it seems as if we don't have believers that are genuinely saved by understanding what faith means. This makes it easy for the devil or world system to interfere. Such people act and make decisions just the way unbelievers do. They do things based on their intellect and rely on their strength. Well, we can simply say that they have a knowledge problem or should we say a faith problem.

Hebrews 11:1 defines faith as "the assurance of things hoped for, the conviction of things not seen." That same chapter goes further to say that the elders of old obtained good reports through faith. They did all kinds of miracles and signs and wonders just by believing in the faith, which was just the substance. If that could be the result of the elders who only have faith as a substance, what do we have to show as a generation privileged to walk in the reality of that faith?

Faith comes by hearing the Word of God. What that means is that when the gospel was taught to us, we accepted it by faith. So it was at that point that faith was established in our hearts. We must allow that faith to be expressive in our dealings, especially as it regards to our daily needs.

God desires for faith to change us. He expects us to renew our minds through and by believing in the Word. Jesus told that to his disciples when he was about to go. He instructed them to abide in the vine and that without him, they could do nothing. However, he emphasized the need to get them purified from the world. But later, he made them realize that the Word they heard had purified them and made them clean. That tells us that part of what God's Word, which inspires faith action, will do is that we will be cleansed and become the way God wants us to be, wanting nothing (John 15:3). With that, we will be conscious of the fact that the essence of faith's reality is that it affects every area of our lives, changing the way we think and behave.

Faith causes us to act on what we have not yet experienced. In Romans 4:17b, the Bible says, "calls into existence the things that do not exist." Ultimately, he wants us to believe that he can bring to fulfillment all the promises of the Scriptures that are yet to manifest in our lives and to trust him even when our situation has not changed.

How Do We Live By Faith and Not By Sight?

The difference between Christians and non-Christians is that while the former live by faith in God, the latter live by sight. Living by faith and not sight, to me, simply means being willing to believe and go into the unknown or unseen. It is about trusting God to lead the way, even though we don't know the outcome. This was the same step Abraham took. The Lord instructed him to leave his father's land for the land he would show him. He also promised he was going to bless him and make him the father of nations. And Abraham acted in faith. He left his father's house to go to a land he had not seen. He knew the Lord would not go back on his word, including making him a father of nations. That is, the Scriptures say, "in hope he believed against hope, that he should become the father of many nations, as he had been told, 'So shall your offspring be." (Rom 4:18). In the following verse 19, the Bible says, "he did not weaken in faith when he considered his own body, which was as good as dead (since he was about a hundred years old), or when he considered the barrenness of Sarah's womb." From the above verse, it is affirmed that Abraham received the promise by believing in what was said concerning him. This was why he never considered the weakness of his body and the deadness of Sarah's womb. James 2:22-23 confirms "that faith was active along with his works, and faith was completed by his works; and the Scripture was fulfilled that says, 'Abraham believed God, and it was counted to him as righteousness"—and he was called a friend of God.'"

If we have been in any situation for any length of time, have been praying over it fervently, and we don't know how it will turn out or when the answer will come, be not afraid. We don't need to focus our minds on how it's going to come. But know that God is working, and we should be patiently waiting to see the outcome. This is not a fun fair; it is a moment when we need to trust that he is in control, and that is where we find peace. The Bible says, "but my righteous one shall live by faith," (Heb 10:38).

Away from living by faith, we have lived by sight. "For we walk by faith, not by sight." (2 Cor 5:7). This means not living by the human five senses. It is not living based on what we can see, feel, touch, smell, and taste. This is the kind of life that ordinary or average men are living until they know Christ. It is being controlled or influenced by what they see or feel. Such men will have to rely on their intellect and wits when they make decisions. They want you to tell them what they see and how real things are and not believe things out of your imagination. But the Bible referred to this as being carnally minded, and the result of such life is death. It is a life that is against the will and purpose of God, and it can never please God.

This is the state of every man when they have not known Christ. It's a normal lifestyle for every unbeliever but abnormal for every Christian. That is why Apostle Paul admonished the Colossian church and, by extension, every one of us to set our affection on things above. We should be conscious of a reality that exists in God more than believing in the physical world.

The truth is the world system and science have done a lot of harm to our faith lives. That's a tragic mistake. Both systems are structured to wipe out God's factor from the equation. We now see the faith life as abnormal or awkward, whereas that is how God wants us to see or approach him. God wants to reward his people based on their faith walk and not how they feel. God is not moved by feelings but by faith.

Unfortunately, we still have believers who have been saved for many years, yet their feelings still control them. This is not a sign of spirituality. We should go a bit higher than ordinary men as believers. Faith goes beyond what can be seen or touched.

Two Paths You Must Not Toil

When it comes to the matter of faith, there are two areas where people are lacking. We have some people who believe that all they need is faith; they don't have to do anything again. We also have people who believe that God will have to show them visible proof before they believe him. Let's discuss one after the other.

Those with the first mindset are similar to those who never had a job. They don't have what God will bless them with, yet all they do is hope that some sort of miracle will happen. God is not a magician. The Bible says he will bless the work of your hands and that your labor will be greatly rewarded. Such instruction, however, is not for someone who does work. In fact, such a person is not acting in faith. Acting in faith means starting something and holding God by his word concerning it. Though we often say faith is deedless, it often shows itself in deeds. It was by deeds Abraham showed that he believed. James 2:26 says, "For as the body apart from the spirit is dead, so also faith apart from works is dead." What that means is that faith without corresponding action will not yield any result. This is why many people are frustrated today.

I believe that most people who leave the faith today do so because of frustration. Maybe they tried all kinds of methods to access God. Maybe they fasted and prayed, and because there were no results, they denounced Christ. That's self-deception anyway. But the truth is that there should be a corresponding action that backs what we believe. This is not to say that God is not in the miracle-working business. I'm saying that when we move, he moves. He isn't going to pour the job on us; but after we apply, make the cakes, and decorate the rooms, he will open the doors to make those dreams become realities.

As Christians, we must align our actions with what is written concerning the matters we are believing God for. Even in science or medicine, they don't just certify a method except if it has been proven effective. I read some time ago that before a drug can be prescribed, it must have passed through four preparatory/ testing stages and been found authentic. Why do you think that is necessary? They know how important life is and the damage an improperly produced drug can cause. As a believer, take steps that match what the Lord has said concerning you. For instance, if the Lord has promised he is going to give you a car, learning how to drive may be the next wise step to take.

Another path we must be wary of as far as faith is concerned is of those who believe that God needs to show them proof before they will believe. They want God to give them signs for almost everything they are expecting from him. These are people that Thomas would relate to.

Well, nothing is bad when God instructs you to do it, and you want to be sure you heard him. But it becomes a lack of faith when you always want him to validate his instruction with signs. In John 20:29, "Jesus said to him, 'Have you believed because you have seen me? Blessed are those who have not seen and yet have believed.'" The scenario of Moses in the book of Exodus, when the Lord told him to go and meet Pharaoh so the people of Israel could be set free, shows that asking for signs is a product of fear and doubt. When the Lord called him and gave him the instruction, he gave a lot of excuses, making God see why he shouldn't be the one to face Pharaoh. From their conversation, you would observe that it took God time to convince Moses to go for the assignment. At one point, Moses had to openly confess that God should send another person. The truth is there are some assignments that God has for us that it only takes faith to act on.

If we ask for signs, we may even get discouraged and confused by them when they arrive. As humans, we tend to question every action of God. We know he is mighty and powerful. We agree that he knows the end from the beginning, but we are too fearful to commit our lives to his hands. That's not good enough. God demands the utmost trust and faith.

Ways Faith Can Practically Change Your Life

If you are doubting how powerful living a faith life can be or you are wondering if your life can experience a turnaround without having to hold to New Age beliefs, perhaps you need to consider the following beneficial things faith will give you.

I.) Faith Produces Strength

When you read strength, don't let your mind go to the physical strength you need to fight battles or bullies. What I mean is an inner resolve to withstand difficult situations. I can tell you that some people subscribe to the New Age philosophies because they think that is what you need. They want a belief that prioritizes human abilities against divine intervention.

In Psalms 138, the Bible says, "In the day when I cried out, you answered me, and made me bold with strength in my soul." When you are right with God, you can do things alone. This is because you have the Creator of the universe on your side.

Consider the example of David and Goliath in 1 Samuel 17. David was a shepherd boy. He was never the strong-warrior type, but when Goliath mocked his God, David required the king to order him to fight him. Where you are now, picture a kid who delivers your papers telling the president, "Let me address this one."

David was not frightened, nor did he lose control because of Goliath's insults or size; instead, he had faith in God. So, he told the giant that the Lord who rescued him from the paw of the lion and the paw of the bear would rescue him from the hand of this uncircumcised Philistine (1 Sam 17:37). David had faith that God would defeat the giant and deliver his people, so he stood for the people and defended the entire Israelites from the insult made against them by the Philistine.

II.) Faith Births Courage

Strength and courage aren't the same, even though they can be synonymous. Courage is the ability to confront what scares us, to act on our beliefs despite imminent danger, and to show strength in the face of grief or pain. Courage, like strength, comes from the understanding of the power of God that is accessed through faith. Our confidence that heaven is real will affect the risks we will take. If death is the end of all things, the worst that can happen to anyone, then what do you do to hurt someone who believes there is a better life after this world? That would definitely be a challenge.

Esther is a perfect example of a courageous person who displayed her virtue to the greatest height. She risked her life because she needed to save her people, not minding what would happen to her if the king was not pleased with her step. At that tumultuous time for the Israelites, Esther risked her life and delivered her people from an evil man's bitter vendetta.

III.) Faith Produces Stability

Have you seen people who seem undisturbed even though there is trouble everywhere? My cousin was unshakable during the heat of the COVID-19 pandemic. She already knew what the Word said concerning her life. The Bible says no weapon formed against me shall prosper. She saw the pandemic as a weapon from the pit of hell to destabilize and instill fear in the minds of believers. Some people never seem to get weary or anxious.

A coworker only takes a deep breath when her system crashes instead of slamming her hands on the desk and starts looking tense or worried—the mom who tries to calm her kid's last-minute requests that are piling up.

Despite how we sometimes feel, we should remain calm and persist throughout the day. We want to pass through the process without melting down under any circumstances. We understand it is almost impossible not to experience challenges, but our heart is established and stabilized in the middle of the difficulties that life throws at us. When we feel in control, we are holding on to the comfort that the Word of God brings.

If we observe the life of Daniel and Joseph in the Bible, we will see that they lived a life of stability despite the many instabilities they faced. They passed through many challenges, yet their experiences and circumstances didn't shape or shift their focus from God. Daniel and other Israelites were captured and forced to join the king's service.

This gave Daniel the privilege of having new clothes, learning new customs and languages, and eating the king's meat. Even though he was a captive, he stayed true to the God of the Hebrews. He wouldn't eat anything the king declared, and God came through for him. He was promoted to the king's royal court, where some individuals didn't like his God but rather the god of the king. They plotted against him, throwing him inside the lion's den, but he stood true to his word and expressed his faith in the God of the Hebrews even when he was held in bondage at Babylon.

Faith is powerful. It can do anything in your life if you let it. It is like a seed that a farmer plants. When it is properly watered, it germinates and produces fruit. When you release your faith in any circumstance, what you are doing is attracting God's power to work, but when you are relying on your wits or science, you are limiting the flow of God. As a result of releasing your faith, you can transform your life and become an extraordinary person, like Abraham, who had his mind fixed on the reality of God's Word more than what the world taught him.

In conclusion, we must know our stance on faith. What exactly do we think faith is? Why is faith important, and can we release our faith to attract the power of God? This is necessary for us to live a victorious life, even as Christians. In faith, there is total relevance. There is absolute confidence in the power of God. You are just confident that he will never leave you nor forsake you. If you understand the unfailing love he has for you, you will understand that he can't deny you in your downtimes. He is more constant and reliable than science and technology. This does not mean that his answer is always yes, but in his own timing, he will answer for our good.

Key Takeaways

- Faith has to do with believing or trusting the Word of God concerning a matter.

- Actions that are birthed when faith is released might not make sense. It also goes against the principles of common sense.

- The difference between Christians and non-Christians is that while the former live by faith, the latter live by sight.

- As far as faith is concerned, God will always answer in his own timing. The answer might not always be yes, but it will be for our good. It might even be greater than what we asked for.

"Don't have just a little vision of what God can do for you. You're not inconveniencing God to believe big. In fact, when you believe to do great things, it pleases God"-Joel Osteen.

Chapter 6

FAITH AND THE CONCERNS OF LIFE

"No matter what has happened to you in the past or what is going on in your life right now, it has no power to keep you from having a perfect future if you will walk by faith in God. God loves you! He wants you to live with victory over sin so you can possess His promises for your life today!"—Joyce Meyer

Life is full of ups and downs. One moment you think you have figured it out, and at a moment's notice, you have just been thrown a curveball. You then begin to wonder where and how you missed it. You have not missed the ball game. But maybe you have not mastered how to keep your faith amid the myriad of challenges that life has thrown at you.

Most times, we are not conscious enough to know that we are not the problem. We are too quick to find faults in ourselves. We have tried everything we could, yet nothing is working the way we want it to. The truth is that we can't keep holding ourselves responsible for the issues we didn't cause. We can't keep blaming ourselves for what nature throws at us. We just have to find an antidote or tool we can use to address all the concerns of life. And that is our faith. At the same time, we must accept responsibility for those things that we did cause. The Bible affirmed that the only victory that has conquered and overcome the world and its concern is that which comes through our faith (1 John 5:4). So, with that, we can be assured that we are on the winning side.

One of the surest things in this life is that we will have one challenge or the other to deal with. And the truth is that we don't have to do anything before they come. Challenges spring up as occasions demand and as life throws them at us. Since there are good times, we should always expect some moments we will not be comfortable with. But when such situations occur, what should we do?

The strongest and most inspiring people in the Christian faith are not those who never face difficulties in life; they are those who learn to stand on the Word regardless of their circumstances. That's why we look at the examples of those that have gone ahead of us in the faith and follow the path written about in Philippians 4:9 which says, "what you have learned[a] and received and heard and seen in me—practice these things, and the God of peace will be with you." When we observe Paul's steps, we will understand that he moved through the same circumstances we are facing now, but Paul never gave up. Instead, he looked up and received help from above. What gave him the ability to stand despite numerous challenges was his conviction and faith in God. Faith-filled conviction in the Word of God produced confidence. This is what Paul taught the church.

It is easy to feel that there is no help or hope in this upside-down world full of failure, disappointment, war, and pain. As Christians, it is hard to find fulfillment in life without putting God first in everything with faith. But amid everything, we must understand how much we are loved.

The love of God can't be compared to that which you share with your spouse, family members, or friends. That kind of love has an inconsistent nature and is often attached to something or a requirement, but God's love is infinite and unconditional. You do nothing to qualify for it, and neither do you need to do anything to keep it. This kind of love won't allow you to go through the storm of life all by yourself. God understands you are naive and that you need him to help you as you make decisions and take steps. That's why he wants us to include him in that plan, so we will always come back to him for instructions when things become difficult.

Right now, everything inside you is making you feel as if all is falling apart, but the never-ending love of God is telling you there is more. Remember how God provided for the Israelites in the Bible. They were working; they had no daily dealings, yet God fed them because of his faithfulness. God's love brings about his faithfulness, and we are saved in his love despite how difficult things seem to be.

God cares about every detail of your life.

There is a part in all men that makes them want to be self-reliant. We say to ourselves, "I achieved all this on my own, without a single person's help." The more usual or smaller the detail is, the greater the desire to rely on self. We tend to think there are parts of our lives that we don't need help with, so we remove God from the equation.

And yet, despite what we tell ourselves, the Scriptures' position is clear. It tells us how God is interested in and cares about every detail of our lives. "Are not two sparrows sold for a penny? And not one of them will fall to the ground apart from your Father. But even the hairs of your head are all numbered." (Mat 10:29–30). Also, in Psalm 37:23, the Psalmist says that "the steps of a man are established by the LORD, when he delights in his way."

God is interested in every single detail of our lives and delights to be part of it if we allow him. That means those little things you think you can handle by yourself; those things that seem like your family or friends can help with; God cares about them all. He cares about how we want to survive this economic crisis. He is concerned about your final paper even if you have not prepared enough.

He cares about the deadline of the job you have not met at work and your children's allergies and sniffles. He wants you to know that the matters that concern your health, finances, purpose, and job concern him too. To put it bluntly, God cares about us, period!

Over time, I have discovered that it is easy to remove God from the equation when we focus on ourselves and on the capacity of mankind. Some people tend to say something like, "Must you spiritualize everything?" And I feel like they don't know how much God cares and is concerned about us. He doesn't just want to be a God we will look up to when we need something; he wants to be the father that he is. The Greek word for the word "father" is *pata*, which means your *source* and *sustainer.*

Today, we have people who are mere fathers only at the level of being a source and not at the level of a sustainer, and that is not what makes a father. If God is indeed the Father, the one whom the Scriptures affirmed to us, then he should be our sustainer. A sustainer cares for and provides for your needs at every turn. As a sustainer, he has every resource that can satisfy us whenever we are in need.

When it comes to explaining how much God cares for us even at a difficult moment in our lives, I usually use the example of a little child and their parents. If you have a little child of about two or three years old, you will understand that they don't care where you get money to get what they need; they just come to you, demanding one thing or the other.

They trust you enough that all their needs will be met. They could care less how, but they just know you can't fail them. And if you are not providing on time, you start seeing them nagging or crying. And then you can't stand it; you just give in. That's the same situation that happens between God and us. When we need things that are hard, we go to God in faith. And when we pray, we should establish a word in our hearts and constantly declare it until we see it come to pass.

Most of the time, believers are not persistent in their petition of prayer. We need something, then we go to God in prayer, and shortly, we are done. Most of us don't even wait to receive an instruction to run with; we just feel like God will do it if he wants to do it. Jesus told us about the power of persistence when we pray. He used the parable of a woman and the judge to illustrate how a believer must be persistent and focused on the things they want God to do. Several times, this woman would go to the judge demanding justice. Her consistency and manner of persistence made the cruel judge have a change of mind, and he granted the woman's request. Though the ears of God are not deaf, nor is his arm too short to save, we can't rule out the place of consistency and persistence in the place of prayer. Apart from bringing our prayer requests to the front, they also build or equip us to be able to grasp all that God has for us.

Yes, there will be ups and downs. This fact has been proven throughout the ages. One day we are smiling and the next day there are tears. Since there is nothing that we can do to prevent these low times, what do we do to get through them? According to songwriters Hoffman and Showalter we are to lean on his everlasting arms. Are we to ask for an appointment to get to these arms? Do we wear long or short sleeves for our appointment with the arms? Will the comfort come from direct skin to skin contact with the arms? No, I think we know by now that this is symbolism for our faith and God's faithfulness. To get comfort from the everlasting arms that we will not see, we must first have faith that they are there and that they will comfort us. His arms are just his presence, his ear and concern, if you will, what we can count on forever.

And what of the section of this hymn that says, "Oh how sweet to walk in this pilgrim way." Walking in a pilgrim way does not refer to walking at all but instead to our lifestyle or very act of being, how we behave. The dictionary refers to a pilgrim as someone on a religious or moral journey and devoted to the belief in the journey.

Abraham was a great example of a pilgrim. His walking the pilgrim way took humility and faith. He was obedient in his walk. So, Abraham walked with humility and faith.

When the trials of life are raging, I happily submit that we should lean on Jesus when:

Enemies - When we have enemies, we are to give these things over to the Lord. Faith dictates that God will take care of it. We are to pray for our enemies and love them the same as everyone else. I believe that we are to try to forget about the misdeed done to us, in that way, God acts (this is just my belief). God will do what should be done to avenge us. We never know, hardship may come to our foes in our lifetimes and sometimes later. Never wish for an enemy's demise though, leave it to God.

Death – We must all face that impending fate of death. If we know that we all must die, why is there so much fear in it? Why is there so much sadness when it happens naturally? The Bible tells us that physical death is not the final chapter. If we live according to the word of the Lord, we have another home not made by man. I must admit that I fear, to a certain degree, the pain of it. I pray to die in my sleep as we all do at some point, I imagine. All these things are out of our hands so why would worrying about them help us? I believe that it takes faith to get to where God wants us concerning death.

Doubt – Doubt can creep in at our most vulnerable moments. I submit that even the strongest person can be hit with moments of doubt. We can doubt our sanity, our health, or anything. When we doubt our faith, we need to reevaluate. Both Thomas and Peter doubted Jesus whom they had seen do wonders. I believe that this can be used by Satan to lead us down the wrong path. When we have doubt, we should seek God and He will carry us through.

Fear of Failure – Mistakes are an inherent part of being human. Some say it wasn't a mistake if you knew you were wrong and did it anyway. Now this is different because I believe they are still mistakes if the person has grief about the action. Some people have grief during and after the action. Paul had grief only after and God still used him. Even Elijah made mistakes as well as Moses, Peter, Abraham, and David. God used their mistakes to show us what not to do and that His love for us is even greater than any mistake we could ever make. God judges the hearts of man. So, if we know all of this, we should know to put our best foot forward and try again when we fall. Yes, it gets hard sometimes but we must get back up again as Pastor Donnie McClurkin puts it. My pastor shows a wonderful illustration of this when he brings in the inflatable punching bag. Each time he hits the bag it comes back to a standing position. We must have faith that God is with us and lean on him. Even though I struggle with this daily even to the point of self-sabotage at times. At this point we might be held hostage to fear and not just fear of failure. I have to lean on God to help me in this area that Satan is all too familiar with. Accepting full responsibility for my actions, I also know that the enemy knows my shortcomings. We all must try, try, and try again to the best of our abilities with the faith that God will see us through. We need to have faith that he is our refuge for whatever fear might befall us.

Addictions – Some of us are prone to certain things more than others. These things can become addictive when we need them to feel normal and we put them before God. When a person is in AA, they are told to avoid relationships for at least a year after treatment. This is because the addictive personality will more than likely replace the substance with the relationship and depend on it for all the good feelings that the object of addiction does. This can lead to codependency and everything else that can take us away from ourselves and God. Another individual should not be so needy until their needs overtake the giver's needs. When these things happen, we look to God to help us. As for myself and my own demons with said subject, I have to realize that I look to God for everything. He supplies all my needs. The word tells me how I am to live. The word also tells me that I am not my own but I belong to the Father and he expects certain things from me. His word also says that we have free will. I believe that Satan uses this part of the word as thorns in our flesh. He also uses our emotions as thorns: guilt, shame, fear, and anger, to get us back into the sinful state. It takes a great amount of faith to withstand the pull of addiction. I believe that this is because we can become so tired of hurting and our addiction is an easy way to feel good again. We can't look for easy fixes. We must seek God in all situations.

We will be tempted to look to other means to help us in any of the concerns of life. If we look hard enough and not allow faith to be intermingled with the beliefs of this world, we can become stronger individuals.

Exercising Faith Amid Everyday Troubles and Emotions

We indeed face a myriad of challenges and emotions daily. The positive side of our emotions produces love, gratitude, joy, and more, while the negative part births disappointment, fear, and anxiety. Though being emotional is not inherently bad, we often find that controlling our emotions is difficult. This gives them the opportunity to dictate our faith life and distract us from him. This is also why we should rely on God's help so that we can fight temptation and put our emotions at bay.

In 2 Corinthians 10:2–3, Apostle Paul emphasizes that though we are humans, we don't fight like humans. In fact, the weapons of our warfare are not made by humans. Rather, they are powerful instruments made by God and vital to pulling down strongholds.

With them, we take captive every thought that negates God's plan to the obedience of Christ. Also, in Ephesians 6:16, Paul said, "in all circumstances take up the shield of faith, with which you can extinguish all the flaming darts of the evil one." In both Scriptures above, Paul emphasizes that spiritual weapons can gain control over human defenses. These human defenses come most often in the form of intellectual arguments, pride, and emotional defenses against the knowledge of Christ.

Basically, there are some thoughts that prevent people from acting in faith. So, you need God's weapon, which is faith, to pull down every stronghold. Also in Ephesians, it tells us that one of these weapons God equipped us with is known as the shield of faith. What that means is that we can imagine the positive outcome of any situation and act as though it was true.

Faith is believing God's Word and following it over our emotions. The reason is, most times, our emotions don't really tell the actual truth that is in our human spirits. That is because they cannot do so. We have to open our spirit and allow it to help our weaknesses rather than allowing the flesh to control our beings. The scripture says sins shall no longer have dominion over us because we are now under the influence of grace. Grace is faith, and faith is strong. We can control ourselves through the strength that is produced by and in the Spirit.

How to Start Building Your Faith

Faith is a journey that involves obeying God's words and taking them as they are. Building a consistent life of faith starts with your daily choice to rely on God for everything. What makes that faith journey starts from making the daily decision to follow God and live by faith rather than being controlled by your emotions. We might be tempted to act or allow our emotions to control us as emotional beings. I believe that having the Word inside us will help us. This is why Paul said let the Word of God dwell in you richly.

The Spirit that dwells inside of us needs to be constantly fed with accurate words of God. It is through that Word we will be able to give accurate responses to everyday challenges that confront us.

Don't forget, Satan wants us to become so distracted and clouded with negative emotions that we believe God to be far away from us. That is simply not the truth that our Bible teaches. It teaches that we are not given the spirit of fear or timidity but of sound mind (2 Tim 1:7). So, we should not allow fear or stress to consume or dictate how we live our lives. Fear and stress both give glory to the devil rather than God.

As we live our lives, we can rest assured that something will give us reason to worry. The truth is, in God's kingdom, it is the accurate application of God's Word that addresses situations and not the application of what we feel can help us through. Feelings are too inconsistent, but God's Word is a never-changing truth that abides for life.

Are you feeling worried or anxious? Think about what the Bible says, "do not be anxious about anything, but in everything by prayer and supplication with thanksgiving let your requests be made known to God. And the peace of God, which surpasses all understanding, will guard your hearts and your minds in Christ Jesus. (Phil 4:6-7). The Bible says that we should choose prayer over fear.

For any scenario that makes us afraid or feel worried, there is a sure word from God that can solve them. But to be consistent with that kind of life, we must start making the right choice of prioritizing and trusting God. The Bible says, "I sought the LORD, and he answered me and delivered me from all my fears. Those who look to him are radiant, and their faces shall never be ashamed. This poor man cried, and the LORD heard him and saved him out of all his troubles." (Ps 34:4–6).

Despite many challenges, fears, and circumstances, David trusted that God would take care of him. Learning to live by faith in our everyday lives starts with understanding the source of our fears. That may seem simple and yet extremely difficult at the same time. If we put our trust in people other than God, anxiety and fear will continue to influence our thoughts. We need to trust God and focus our attention and efforts on things that build our faith in God daily.

Trust God Too Much to Give Up

When you are at the worst moment, why should you trust God? Many believers ask me that question when the subject of faith is brought up. And my sincere answer has been that God can turn the situation around for you. I wasn't saying that to make them feel that they have not trusted God enough for the kind of result they want but to stir up faith in them so much that they will see their situations as something God can handle.

I hope you understand that God is more interested and would like to help you even in that irrelevant matter. The truth is don't expect God to show up on big matters when you neglect him in small matters. It bothers me how people who never received any instruction from God before choosing the course they studied in school, never got a go-ahead from God on the job they are doing right now, suddenly want God to intervene when it comes to marital or financial issues. I'm sure God must have been speaking on the matter concerning their lives since the very day they became born again, but because they had no clues of how God operates, they missed out on his plan for them.

You must trust God's Word enough not to give up. We can rest assured that the words spoken concerning us will not return void. They must accomplish that which they were set to do in our lives. Holding God to his word brings him to action.

Fainting in troubled times shows doubt and insecurity. Fainting or losing hope when you are in your own moment shows that your strength is small. And that shows you have not been feeding on God's Word enough to get sustained by it. It also shows you have not been feeding on the accurate Word of God because you must have read that days of trials and temptations are inevitable. That means you should prepare for these kinds of moments instead of getting weary and weak along the way.

It is quite dangerous for armies to go to the war front without weapons and competencies. They will just be vulnerable and defenseless. We should also be conscious of the fact that as believers, this world is a battlefield. You either lose or win. What determines whether you are going to be victorious or not is what you are standing on. The firm foundation of the Lord is key. Make sure that your anchor holds and grips this solid rock.

If God has spoken a word to you concerning that situation, it is better to hold on to it. God's words are ever sure; though it looks like nothing is happening, I can assure you that God is working. You will be amazed when you see that the Lord is working everything out in your favor, and I'm sure he will be glorified in your life now and eternally.

Key Takeaways

- Life is full of ups and downs; it is not stable, but God's words are.

- The strongest and most inspiring people in the Christian faith are not those who never face difficulties in life; they are those who learn to stand on the Word regardless of their circumstances.

- Faith is a journey that involves obeying God's words and taking them as they are. Building a consistent life of faith starts with your daily choice to rely on God for everything.

- There is a part in every man that always makes them feel the need to be self-reliant.

- As long as we put our trust in people other than God, anxiety and fear continue to influence our thoughts.

Chapter 7

OUR FAITH AND GOD'S FAITHFULNESS

"Our faith is not meant to get us out of a hard place or change our painful condition. Rather, it is meant to reveal God's faithfulness to us in the midst of our dire situation."—David Wilkerson

One lovely longtime childhood friend once asked me to hypothetically choose between never seeing her again but keeping the memories we shared or being together as much as we wanted but forgetting her daily. The options she presented were dicey. I don't know what inspired it, but I found it intriguing.

After thinking for a while, I chose the former option because I thought it would be better to always remember her than to forget her daily life. This question, however, made me understand the value of memories. I understood that without memories, we don't know who we are and how valuable we are in the lives of people around us. Good memories are records of our lives and proof of our existence. We should not get this confused with looking back at negative things that God has brought us through.

But unfortunately, memory is imperfect; and over time, we are prone to forget things easily. It puts us in a position where we forget God's faithfulness over our lives or begin to compare human faithfulness with the faithfulness of God.

For someone who has been jilted, the gospel of faithfulness or being faithful will likely be the last thing they want to hear. I think the first mistake people make is to think or equate God's faithfulness with that of humans. They fail to realize that human beings are frail and prone to errors. They can make promises and change their minds. God is ever faithful irrespective of human shortcomings.

Over time, I have discovered two reasons why men easily forget how faithful God is—first, they tend to equate and misconstrue God's character with human nature, and second, they tend to forget how tremendous God's faithfulness has been displayed across ages and dispensations.

Take, for example, the people of Israel. While they were in Egypt, God saw the kind of pain and agony they were passing through; and in his bid to save them, he wrought many wonders, signs, and miracles that wowed many nations, including the children of Israel themselves. But when they got to the wilderness, where their faith in Yahweh was tested, they forgot how gracious he had been to them simply because of food. And consequently, their faith was shipwrecked, and they started doubting the God of their fathers.

When you read that story today, you probably feel ashamed and shake your head in disbelief at the Jewish people's lack of faith. You wonder aloud, "How could they not trust God enough to supply food despite his display of wonderful power?" But are we better now?

Do you not often do the same as the Israelites?

When we are in our downtime, we ask God to help us, he hears our prayers, and his perfect timing comes through for us. But as soon as we face another struggle, we quickly forget how gracious God had been to us. And because of that, we worry and complain about his character. We think he is too slow; perhaps he could be a bit faster.

But in an actual sense, we are faithless. This is the will of God for us. He wants us to remember him even when the victory is unsure.

Today, when bad things happen to us believers, we tend to go overboard and start questioning where God is as though he has changed position. Maybe we need to keep a journal to keep track of what God is doing in our lives. We should begin with gratitude for the air we inhale and exhale daily. Then we can move to the daily provision of God and think about those who have been hospitalized. Is God really faithful?

Let's Be Clear

Our understanding of God's faithfulness will be enhanced when we see it from the angle of a person's faithfulness. The level of someone's faithfulness is measured by their capacity to hold you up or support you when his help is needed. If you want pictorial evidence, you can think of pillars supporting a structure. A person's faithfulness is measured by the degree to which he can provide the bedrock for his faith. Have you trusted friends with a secret because they gave you a reason to do so? They made themselves worthy of that, remember? You didn't just decide to share a secret. You have tested and proven them worthy. You know any private information you share with them will remain the way you want. They gave you a solid bedrock for your conviction.

In that way, they are found trustworthy or "faithful." This is what they have demonstrated in the past, so you believe they would do more because of the track record of their faithfulness. So that past record provides a solid conviction for your faith. If they could do it then, they should be able to do so now.

This is how it works between you and God. God's track record of faithfulness gives you a conviction for exercising faith. God's action solidifies your faith and strengthens your conviction, even in times of trouble. We believe that a building with strong and supporting pillars can't fall, so when you act on God's proven Word, it didn't fail then so you believe it won't fail now.

What's More About God's Faithfulness?

You must have heard or read the portion of the Bible that says that God is not a man that he should lie, nor a son of man that he should repent (Num 23:19). When you read that, what comes to your mind?

Repentance?

Yes, when God makes promises, he can't be threatened to change them. No one can coerce him to make a U-turn on his promises concerning you. What he says he will do is the exact thing he will do. That's God's faithfulness on display. When God makes a promise, most of the time, he doesn't depend on human effort to carry it out because he knows how inconsistent we can be at times. So, he ensures all things are made perfect by him and through him.

Because of the fall of man, we are being taught to believe what we can see and not what we can't see. If God tells you he will bless you, you will probably ask for signs. You want God to prove that he can do what he has promised. I have seen people threaten God with their prayer points. Some people will say, "God, I need you to show up for the last time; else, I will stop serving you." First, you must understand that God doesn't need you; somehow, he wants you. That is why he prepared salvation for you from the foundation of the world. He wanted you to come into the place of fellowship to satisfy your desire or quest for a supernatural being.

As I said, human beings love proof. They seek them before any message from God can be validated, but I hope you understand that God's faithfulness will not allow him to make promises he can't fulfill. That will make him less than the God he is, and that is impossible.

Rest in God's Faithfulness, Not Yours

"Do your best to present yourself to God as one approved, a worker who has no need to be ashamed, rightly handling the word of truth." (2 Tim 2:13).

This scripture accurately describes a radical way of living, not the use of our natural senses. Most believers subscribe to the view that life is your shoulder. You can make or break your life, and you have no one to blame for your misfortune but yourself. This view has to do with mastering your life and fate. You have little to rely on other than your senses, wisdom, and strength that you have gathered over the years. It is all about you trying to fix everything all by yourself and for yourself. It is you against the wicked world. That was your former life until you came into Christ, an entirely different kind of being.

You are now in God's kingdom, where you not only are welcomed into eternal glory but also have a seat in eternity. A standard of living is about submitting to God's will and moral code. It is also the kind of living where God covenanted and committed himself to be faithful to you forever. He unleashes his power, wisdom, and grace to run the race of life without scars.

One of the most intriguing things about the faithfulness of God is that he can be trusted when you cannot. Have you been in a situation where you have come to the end of your wits? Remember, you never imagined God could come through for you. You were so helpless, defenseless, and powerless. Still, God showed up. He did that because he couldn't depend on your faith at that time to act.

One thing I have noticed about God is that he can do anything to protect his nature. He can do anything to show you that he is ever faithful. Do you remember that scary nightmare you had?

You thought that calamity would strike after a few days or months, but nothing happened. That is nothing, but God happened.

His faithfulness is vividly evident in his relationship with the people of Israel. God made a land covenant with Abraham, their father, and he never withdrew the promises he made. "Know therefore that the LORD your God is God, the faithful God who keeps covenant and steadfast love with those who love him and keep his commandments, to a thousand generations," (Deut 7:9). When you consider how God remained unmoved despite their shortcomings, you will understand how much God is faithful to his promises for you that is under his new covenant.

If you have a child around you or have one yourself, a statement like "But you promised!" would not be new to you. Our memories are not as acute as that of a child, and they can be deeply disappointed when we forget things, we promised them. Let's say you promised you were going to buy them toys. They are excited and would be expecting them as promised. But because you have a lot of things in your mind, you forget, and then they feel you don't want to buy toys as promised. All children want promises to be kept by their loved ones. They want to trust that their loved ones will do as they promised. But while we forget, they don't forget.

That is the same with God. It may be possible that we don't even remember most of the promises God has made to us. But he keeps his Word. When he makes a promise, he delivers. In fact, God's faithfulness is foundational to our faith. If we can't trust God for what he said concerning himself and what he did, we have no reason to believe in what he has yet to do in our lives. But because he was able to accomplish all he promised in the Bible, we have reasons to believe that he will fulfill whatever he promised.

A popular Gospel song says, "All the promises of God in Christ are yes and amen." The Bible closely mirrors this in 2 Corinthians

1:20— : "For all the promises of God find their Yes in him. That is why it is through him that we utter our Amen to God for his glory." All that God said concerning actual deliverance, redemption, and the eternal glory are manifested in Christ. And if he could raise Christ from the dead in fulfillment of the prophecies spoken in sundry times about salvation, we have no reason to doubt that he will supply all our needs according to his riches in glory.

Ways God Is Faithful When Life Doesn't Seem Fair

Despite having our shares in the unstable and evolving situations that life brings, God still remains faithful to his promises concerning us. As humans, we can make promises and forget to fulfill them.

Life can be hard and challenging, especially when you have tried every option to get out of a "ditch" and every effort proved futile. You then wonder, what is next? But many thanks to God for those moments when he never turned us down. He knew we were helpless without him, and so he decided to show us faithfulness that is unconditional and stable.

Without faith, it is easy to become cynical and dismiss how God has come through for you in the past, most especially when it looks like you are in the midst of the storm alone. But God is there with you like he was with his disciples. They never thought their master could calm the sea. They never thought winds could obey his command, but when they saw, their perception of the power of God shifted.

God Is Faithful in Helping You Grow Financially

One of the major areas where people lose faith and doubt God is in the provision of finances. We want to make sure that we are not trying to use God as a prosperity God. Yes, he does not want his children to wait until they get to heaven to see all the riches that he can provide for them, but Satan also understands that human beings want more out of life than just survival. In fact, New Age philosophies have taught us that we can create everything we want or need with supernatural but not God's help. That is pure deception. And imaginably, this same belief is now rampant in churches today. Even if you get your daily meal through your hard-earned money, you should understand it is still the same God that enhances your effort. Manifestation can happen through God only and through faith in God. Some people call on Mother Nature or the universe; some say it is the same as God, but I find it to be a very slippery slope.

The Bible says, "you shall remember the LORD your God, for it is he who gives you power to get wealth, that he may confirm his covenant that he swore to your fathers, as it is this day." (Deut 8:18). That scripture confirms that it is only by God's faithfulness that you can receive the power to make wealth "and my God will supply every need of yours according to his riches in glory in Christ Jesus. (Phil 4:19).

Remember earlier when I said that you must be careful? Sometimes, we can become so consumed with trying to become successful that we put God on the backburner. We must always remember that Matthew 6:33 says, "but seek first the kingdom of God and his righteousness, and all these things will be added to you."

God is faithful to encourage and comfort you in your downtimes.

When we are working to get where we need to be financially, there will be times that will test our faith in God concerning these matters. When Paul faced strict persecution and suffering from the enemy of the gospel, he resolved that only God could comfort a believer who faced many challenges; he said "blessed be the God and Father of our Lord Jesus Christ, the Father of mercies and God of all comfort, (2 Cor 1:3).

Paul made this statement when he wasn't sure he was going to live again because of the persecution he faced. This might also apply to you at this moment. You think you have come to the end of the road, and nothing seems to work again, but God's faithfulness would not allow you to go down the drain just like that. With God, there is an ever-present help. You need it now and forever.

God's Faithfulness Strengthens You

"But he said to me, my grace is sufficient for you, for my power is made perfect in weakness. Therefore, I will boast all the more gladly of my weaknesses, so that the power of Christ may rest upon me." (2 Cor 12:9). Many times, we think we are helpless. We often assume that God is far from us and that we lack the strength to tarry a bit longer. In fact, we might have heard words or sermons that depleted our effort and made us weak, yet God is saying his strength is made perfect in our weakness. What that means is that when you think there is less hope for you, God is saying he will bring you to the point that you will marvel at the kind of strength that will come upon you.

I have learned from the Bible and life experiences that we receive God's strength even when we are not prepared for it. Imagine after trying to get this particular job for many years, when you feel that you are tired and can't continue, you receive an offer letter from that company you have been eyeing for a long time. It happened to me, and I'm sure you are next in line to testify.

In conclusion, our faith and God's faithfulness are two separate things. Ours is conditional; it requires us to act or do something before we can attract what we need. But it isn't the same for God's faithfulness. God breathes and protects his Word; he ensures that we are blessed with the Word regardless of our shortcomings. We don't do anything to deserve God's faithfulness. Faithfulness is God's character.

Key Takeaways

- One of the most intriguing things about the faithfulness of God is that he can be trusted when you cannot.

- God's track record of faithfulness gave you a conviction to exercise faith.

- As humans, we can make promises and forget to fulfill them. But for God, fulfillment is in his mind even before he makes any promise.

HOW TO INCREASE YOUR FAITH

If you have found Jesus and are being called out of the New Age to follow him, you may feel confused. You may feel intimidated. If you are just a regular person with no belief system and want to choose God as your personal Savior, you might not know where to begin. You might feel intimidated or embarrassed if you were a strong or outspoken nonbeliever. What would people think? You will have to learn how to increase your faith.

You need to remember that Christianity is rooted in the principles of repentance, forgiveness, and restitution. So, it doesn't matter what you have done; there is always room for you with God. And one of the best things is that the Father will not reject you when you call on him. He understands your areas of weaknesses and strengths.

If you have decided to follow Jesus, the way, the truth, and the life, then do all you can to stay on the journey of faith.

Get on Your Knees (in Other Words, Pray)

The Bible tells us that Jesus "would withdraw to desolate places and pray." (Luke 5:16). This tells me that if the Son often prayed, then we should make prayer a priority in our own lives. We need prayer to communicate with God. We also need prayer to sustain us in everyday life and during times of trouble. I believe the Lord hears the prayers of the righteous. I believe that God meets us where we are. This means don't wait until you are clean to come to the Lord. If you are serious about changing your life, God will help you change it. So, if where you are is not knowing how to pray, then just talk to God, he already knows. He wants us to tell Him all about our lives, good and bad. Like the old song goes - have a little talk with Jesus, tell him all about our troubles and he will answer by and by. I also believe that there is also a way to pray when we want to come correctly to the Father. What I mean is when we want to give it our very best shot.

1.   What is Your Prayer Posture?

It is perfectly fine to pray wherever and however you want. And no, you don't have to be on your knees. There will be times when you want to lean towards formality more than everyday conversational prayer. There will be times when there will be something so serious that you want to give your very best. This is when we need to mind our prayer posture. At these times we should kneel before God. When we kneel, we are showing submission to God and His authority. We also bow our heads for the same reason. Some people lift their heads upward to show that God is higher than we are. I believe it shows even greater submission when we lay prostrate before the Lord. The Bible gives some good examples of this. When Abraham was communicating with the Lord and the Lord made his covenant with him, he "fell on his face." before the Lord. (See Genesis 17:1-22.) This act signifies total submission to the Lord. We do it when we are in dire need of God.

2.   Who is being referenced?

I believe that we should show **reverence when referring to God**, which is a deep respect for Him when we are praying. For instance, in The Lord's Prayer Jesus references God reverently twice. He begins with, "Our Father in heaven, hallowed be your name," (Matt 6:9) The term hallowed means holy. So, Jesus is referencing the

Father as Holy. He is known by many other names, but I believe that we should reference him by what he means to each of us personally.

3.   Do You Have an Attitude of Thanksgiving?

Because the Father has been so good to us, we should take time to tell him just how grateful we are. He is so faithful to us that I find it difficult not to tell him daily. There are so many things that we could list to let the Father know that we are so thankful to him for. From waking us up in the mornings to providing our daily bread. There are so many people who have testified that their prayers were answered faster or with added extras when they showed sincere gratitude.

4.   When Did You Last Ask for Forgiveness?

Just as we must be right with God before we accept communion, the same holds true for prayer. We should repent of our sins. We must tell the Lord that we repent. This means that we are sorry for having sinned. We must then ask to be forgiven. In addition to my repentance, I also must ask God for his forgiveness. Because we are sometimes unaware of some of the things that we may say or do, we should take it a step further. What I mean is that we should ask God to forgive us of sins known and unknown or say I repent of all sins known and unknown.

5.   How do You Ask For Your Needs?

I start off by praying for others. I ask God to help those who are less fortunate than myself. I ask God to help those who don't know him for the pardon of their sins. I ask for the sick to be healed if it is your will. After I have done this which shows concern for others, I ask for myself and my family, church, pastor, job, etc. I always add the statement; not my will but thy will be done. This shows that he holds the final say and that I respect that fact.

What you do here is confess both your known and unknown sins to God. Apologize and pray for forgiveness. The Bible says he is a just and forgiving God. He will forgive you of all the contrary views you held against him. And then pray for the strength to leave behind sins and idols that may have replaced God in your heart. There is no "one-size-fits-all" script for these kinds of prayers. Just ensure it is coming from within your heart. When you do, never doubt if God will forgive you. His Word says he will, so don't allow that doubt to fill your mind. We must pray God's word's to him. For example: You said in your word Lord that where two or more people are gathered together in my name you are in the midst. We ask that you please move on us Lord.

Words of Faith

Since prayer is direct communication with God, our prayers must reflect our faith. We cannot say that we don't think it is going to happen, but I want to ask you for healing in my finger. What I am saying is that our prayer life must be filled with faith. We must believe in what we are saying. Faith in our prayer life opens a whole new subject concerning the tongue. Charles Capps authored a book in the late 70's called 'The Tongue- a creative force.' The premise of the book speaks to the fact that we are made in the image of God. That being the case, we have that same creative force inside us. God has power that comes out of his mouth. He spoke and there was light. He speaks and things happen. In order for the case concerning the tongue to work there has to be faith. I remember the "speak things into existence" era. It is still in existence today and practiced in many faith churches. I submit to you there is nothing wrong with this, in fact it is what God wants. "Truly, truly, I say to you, whoever believes in me will also do the works that I do; and greater works than these will he do, because I am going to the Father. Whatever you ask in my name, this I will do, that the

Father may be glorified in the Son. If you ask me anything in my name, I will do it." (John 14:12-14).

I believe that Jesus wants us to be able to do exactly what he said we should be able to do. "And Jesus answered, 'O faithless and twisted generation, how long am I to be with you? How long am I to bear with you? Bring him here to me.'" (Matt 17:17). Jesus was telling the men to bring the boy who was filled with demons to him. Even though they should have fasted and prayed to cast this demon out Jesus still admonished them for not having the faith to do so. On the ship during the storm, the disciples woke Jesus from his sleep because they were afraid. "Why are you afraid, O you of little faith?" (Matt 8:26a).

If we don't have this kind of faith yet believe that it is within our grasp, we need only to develop our faith by hearing. We all know what the Bible says about faith and how it is obtained. I believe that through faith all things are possible. Let us begin to believe that we can speak a thing into existence. Sometimes they might not come overnight and sometimes they might not come for a while, but we should never stop believing. I believe that God wants to test our faith when he waits a long time. Some people tend to give up on their dreams and their faith after one or two tries. God wants to know how badly you want this and he wants to know that you believe it should be yours.

The Bible says that the word is "life to those who find them, and healing to all their flesh." (Prov 4:22). The word also says that, "you are snared in the words of your mouth," (Prov 6:2). To me this means that our words can either make us or break us. "Death and life are in the power of the tongue," (Prov 18:21a). So let us speak words that are filled with faith over our lives and forsake all words that have negative connotations.

I submit that if we learn to master our faith-filled words that will be able to harness healing and goodwill on Earth just as God planned it. We are his children, and we should have faith that can do all good works - the God kind.

Read the Bible Daily

When you study God's Word diligently, you will become more knowledgeable. Knowledge of any subject gives confidence. Pray to God for the Holy Spirit to direct your heart into the truth of God's Word. Feed your heart and mind with accurate words of God. If your mind is devoid of God's Word, you might be drawn into all types of ungodly beliefs and practices.

Reading your Bible is also a way of giving sacrifice to the Lord. We are sacrificing our time when we read the Bible. Although we don't have to give sacrifices anymore as described in the Old Testament, God still wants our time. As I mentioned earlier, it is a way to communicate with the Lord.

The Bible says, "keep your heart with all vigilance, for from it flow the springs of life." (Prov 4:23). One way you can do that is to download the free ESV Bible app on your phone and/or computer and listen to it. It is helpful every time if you don't have a hard copy of the Bible, and it can be a convenience for you. You should have your own Bible in one of these translations: NASB, NKJV, or ESV, which are, to my knowledge, accurate formal translations.

Get Solid Bible Commentaries to Help You Understand the Bible

While it is good to read the Bible, it would be best if you could get some Bible commentary websites to enhance your understanding. Some helpful commentary authors are Matthew Henry, David

Guzik, and Charles Spurgeon. If you want to use online sources, you can use a website like *GotQuestions.org* and *EnduringWord. com*. They are helpful free websites you can leverage on for a better understanding of any portion of the Bible.

Become an Active Member of a Local Church

Hebrews 10:25 says, "not neglecting to meet together, as is the habit of some, but encouraging one another, and all the more as you see the Day drawing near." So, you need to find a church that teaches sound doctrine and become a full-fledged member. *MichelleLesley. com* can help you find one near you.

Listen to or Watch Online Bible Studies with Respected Teachers

People like Costi Hinn, David Guzik, John MacArthur, Abel Damina, and Cherub Obadare are excellent teachers of God's Word; you can listen to them and watch their Bible study sessions online. Once you begin watching maybe TBN, the Word Network, Daystar, etc. you will be able to figure out which ones you are more comfortable with. They will speak to your soul so to speak.

Delete All Worldly, Messages, and Music

You need to let go of anything that reminds you or connects you with New Age groups or people. It is not enough to just denounce their practice. You must also ensure that you no longer read their books or listen to their tapes. Remove yourself from all their social media sites and replace them with good Christian messages and music. Remember, we only need to have faith in God. There is no need to do anything extra that may jeopardize our relationship with God. It is important to be careful of what we let in our ear gates and eye gates. This means watch what we listen to and look at.

Join a Prayer and/or Bible Study Group

There are a lot of Christian communities where you can learn and grow. If you are involved or a member of a church, they will more than likely have this already. If not, when you visit a church, you may inquire about it. Sometimes Bible study groups and times will be listed online under the names of churches.

Find a Mentor

The impact of discipleship on Christian growth and spiritual maturity can never be overemphasized. It would help if you had someone you could cry to—someone whose footprints cannot be easily erased with the sands of time. When you find someone who is respected for their moral, physical, and spiritual conduct, submit to their leadership. They will help you grow.

Reach Out for Help

As you take the step back to faith, there are some related issues that you are likely going to face. Persecution, loneliness, and being shunned might be part of them. You can receive help to deal with these issues by praying to God for help. Then take the bold step of speaking to a mature Christian friend or pastor about what you are going through. They will advise you on how you can handle such issues.

For everyone who chooses to live the life of victory that we have through Christ, such New Age influences have no power over them. The mighty power of God shields them against any form of satanic influence and power.

So, if you discover that you are obsessed or have been engrossed with anything that is not of the Lord, kindly apply the above steps, and trace yourself back to the faith. God is always willing to have you in his fold. He is a forgiving God and will come and get you just as the good shepherd will leave his ninety-nine sheep to find the one who is lost. He wants to have us back when we fall. He wants to give us another chance and yet another chance to get it right and find where we are loved. We are never too far away from the Lord too far away from salvation. I have heard testimonies of him even forgiving some Satan worshippers.

Have Patience

Anxiety will not stop the seconds from ticking by nor the minutes or hours from doing their perspective jobs. While I remember everything I enjoy and some things I take for granted, I will remain grateful, and I will wait.

CONCLUSION

If you couldn't have imagined holding one or more of the New Age beliefs, that's fine. You are a new being now, and I can feel the moment of joy and fresh hope you are experiencing right now. One thing I have learned in life, especially concerning the journey of my faith, is that the devil will always instigate tricks and devices against me. I hope you know that as well. It is good because the Bible affirms that.

We are made in the image of the true and living God. Now that is truly something to brag about. God wants us to be able to speak things into existence. He wants us to be able to do even greater wonders than he did when he was on the earth.

Now that you know or are now aware that you once held onto one of these beliefs against your Maker, it is vital you turn over a new leaf and make your Christian journey more practical, living from the point of victory that Christ has bought for you. Get acquainted with the study of the Bible and know God for yourself so you won't get entangled with the winds of doctrinal imbalances again. I have much joy and confidence that you are blessed indeed. Remain so. Shalom!

RESOURCES

Gospel of the Descent of the Kingdom (2020). "What Is True Faith? How to Have True Faith in God" retrieved from https://www. holyspiritspeaks.org/testimonies/have-true-faith-in-God/?gclid= Cj0KCQjwsrWZBhC4ARIsAGGUJuqbrFygW14vGqwtejCoPSCa zjI3htt5InGBEJN0KbUoYFE2dE8avIsaAikFEALw_wcB.

Zúme Training. "Faithfulness is Better Than Knowledge"retrieved from https://zume.training/faithfulness-is-better-than-knowledge/.

Eastern Lightning. "The Principles of Relying on God and Looking Up to Him" retrieved from https://en.easternlightning.org/ principles -of-depending-on-god-and-looking-to-god-in-all-things. html?gclid=Cj0KCQjwsrWZBhC4ARIsAGGUJuphqYjJ12CUse2 krpnvIXSOLgv wKroCwORSG8 P3Si7Z8eZSOr8JYa AsfxEALw_wcB.

Broadview Baptist Church. "God's faithfulness versus our faith" retrieved from https://broadview.church/our-faith-gods -faithfulness/.

Tiny Rituals (2022). "New Age Philosophy Explained: Your Guide To New Age" retrieved from https://tinyrituals.co/blogs/tiny-rituals/new-age-philosophy?gclid=Cj0KCQjwsrWZBhC4ARIsAG GUJuoA5ZbGe2hytXON7wV61iriibCAWZ5tEV6gv1Da0CGhJM SmPDVWE saAsETEALw_wcB.

Charles Capps (1976). The Tongue A Creative Force. Harrison House. Tulsa Ok.

Barbara Curtis (2008). "What is 'New Age' Religion, and Why Can't Christians Get on Board?" retrieved from https://www.crosswalk.com/faith/spiritual-life/what-is-new-age-religion-and-why-cant-christians-get-on-board-11573681.html.

Claire Gecewicz (2018). "'New Age' beliefs common among both religious and nonreligious Americans" retrieved from https://www.pewresearch.org/fact-tank/2018/10/01/new-age-beliefs-common-among-both-religious-and-nonreligious-americans/#:~:text=But%20many%20Christians%20also%20hold,unaffiliated%20also%20have%20these%20beliefs.

David Wilkerson-Qoutefancy. Retrieved from: https://www.quotefancy.com/quote/14969617/David-Wilkerson-Our-faith-is-not-meant-to-get-us-out-of-a-hard-place-or-change-our

Doreen Virtue (2020). "10 Guidelines for when Jesus calls you out of the New Age" retrieved from https://doreenvirtue.com/2020/10/20/10-guidelines-for-when-jesus-calls-you-out-of-the-new-age/.

Dolores Cannon (2019). "Three waves of Volunteers" retrieved from https://www.dolorescannon.com.

Joel Osteen (2015). Daily Readings from You can You Will. 90 devotions to becoming a Winner. Faith Words. Hatchett Book Group. New York, New York.

Bruce Wilkinson (2001). Secrets of the Vine. Multnomah Publisher Inc. Sisters Oregon.

Joyce Meyer. Brainy Quotes. Retrieved from:https://www.brainyquotes.com/quotes/joyce_meyer_565139

Nancy Guthrie (2011). Abundant Life. 365 Blessings to begin your day. Tyndale. Carol Stream Illinois.

Dr. Frederick K.C.Price (1976). How Faith Works. Harrison House. Tulsa, Ok.

Rick Warren (2002). The Purpose Driven Life. What on Earth Am I Here For. Zondervan. Grand Rapids, Michigan.